SPEECH AND LANGUAGE-BASED INTERACTION WITH MACHINES:
Towards the Conversational Computer

ELLIS HORWOOD BOOKS IN INFORMATION TECHNOLOGY
General Editor: Dr. JOHN M. M. PINKERTON, Principal, McLean Pinkerton Associates, Surrey, (formerly Manager of Strategic Requirements, ICL)
A PRACTICAL APPROACH TO EXPERT SYSTEMS IN BUSINESS
M. BARRETT, Expertech Limited, Slough, and A. BEEREL, Lysia Limited, London
ELECTRONIC DATA PROCESSING, Vols. 1 and 2*
M. BECKER, R. HABERFELLNER and G. LIEBETRAU, Zurich, Switzerland
EXPERT SYSTEMS: Strategic Implications and Applications
A. BEEREL, Lysia Limited, London
SOFTWARE ENGINEERING ENVIRONMENTS, Vol. 1
P. BRERETON, Department of Computer Science, University of Keele
SMART CARDS: Their Principles, Practice and Applications*
R. BRIGHT, Information Technology Strategies International Limited, Orpington, Kent
PRACTICAL MACHINE TRANSLATION*
D. CLARKE and U. MAGNUSSON-MURRAY, Department of Applied Computing and Mathematics, Cranfield Institute of Technology, Bedford
KNOWLEDGE-BASED SYSTEMS: Implications for Human–Computer Interfaces
D. CLEAL, PA Computers and Telecommunications, London, and N. HEATON, HUSAT Research Centre, Loughborough University of Technology
KNOWLEDGE-BASED EXPERT SYSTEMS IN INDUSTRY
J. KRIZ, Head of AI Group, Brown Boveri Research Systems, Switzerland
INFORMATION TECHNOLOGY: An Overview*
J. M. M. PINKERTON, McLean Pinkerton Associates, Esher, Surrey
EXPERT SYSTEMS IN THE ORGANISATION*
S. SAVORY, Nixdorf Computers AG, FRG
BUILDING EXPERT SYSTEMS: Cognitive Emulation
P. E. SLATTER, Product Designer, Telecomputing plc, Oxford
SPEECH AND LANGUAGE-BASED COMMUNICATION WITH MACHINES: Towards the Conversational Computer*
J. A. WATERWORTH and M. TALBOT, Human Factors Division, British Telecom Research Laboratories, Ipswich

* In preparation

SPEECH AND LANGUAGE-BASED INTERACTION WITH MACHINES:
Towards the Conversational Computer

Editor:
JOHN A. WATERWORTH, B.A., Ph.D.
Research Psychologist
Human Division, British Telecom Research Laboratories, Martlesham Heath

Special Consultant Editor:
Professor JOHN CAMPBELL
Department of Computer Science
University College London

ELLIS HORWOOD LIMITED
Publishers · Chichester

Halsted Press: a division of
JOHN WILEY & SONS
New York · Chichester · Brisbane · Toronto

First published in 1987 by
ELLIS HORWOOD LIMITED
Market Cross House, Cooper Street,
Chichester, West Sussex, PO19 1EB, England
The publisher's colophon is reproduced from James Gillison's drawing of the ancient Market Cross, Chichester.

Distributors:

Australia and New Zealand:
JACARANDA WILEY LIMITED
GPO Box 859, Brisbane, Queensland 4001, Australia

Canada:
JOHN WILEY & SONS CANADA LIMITED
22 Worcester Road, Rexdale, Ontario, Canada

Europe and Africa:
JOHN WILEY & SONS LIMITED
Baffins Lane, Chichester, West Sussex, England

North and South America and the rest of the world:
Halsted Press: a division of
JOHN WILEY & SONS
605 Third Avenue, New York, NY 10158, USA

British Library Cataloguing in Publication Data
Speech and language-based interaction with machines:
towards the conversational computer. —
(Ellis Horwood books in information technology)
1. Automatic speech recognition
I. Waterworth, John A.   II. Talbot, Mike
006.4'54   TK7882.S65
Library of Congress Card No. 87–27558

ISBN 0–7458–0146–3 (Ellis Horwood Limited)
ISBN 0–470–21033–8 (Halsted Press)

Printed in Great Britain by Unwin Bros., Woking

Contents

Preface

This book has its origins in a programme of work conducted at British Telecom Research Laboratories, aimed at developing easily usable, intelligent systems, based on human-computer interaction via spoken and written language, particularly the former. This involved the authors, as members of the Human Factors Division, in conducting a series of experiments designed to answer questions about what types of behaviour an intelligent system with these characteristics should display, and how these might best be achieved.

The book provides a fairly comprehensive account of our work over the last couple of years on speech-based interaction with machines, as well as more recent forays into the area of natural language processing (NLP). NLP is clearly an increasingly important topic of study for a range of Information Technology (IT) applications, including speech-based interaction, and is now the main focus of our work. This volume presents some background issues in the area, which lays the foundation for our current NLP research. We hope to produce a future volume focussing more exclusively on NLP issues - moving from the utterance level to the text/discourse level of processing. All our work is founded on the idea that systems should cater for the needs of their users and not vice versa. In the case of interacting with a source of information via speech, we believe the model of human conversation provides the best approach. The to and fro of conversational interaction is so central to speech communication, and is so deeply entrenched in human behaviour, that it is unavoidable. The conversational computer is definitely coming (albeit slowly). We are some way down the long road towards knowing what that involves, in terms of interactional capabilities. This book is an account of our journey so far.

Many people helped carry out this work, although only two names appear on the cover. Thanks are due to Stephen Furner and John Miles of BTRL, and visiting students Cathy Thomas, Wendy Holmes, and Jean Page, for significant contributions to the experimental work reported. Additional support came from Graham Sherris, for getting the computer to do what we wanted, and to Nicholas Lawson-Williams and Dr Nick Milner, for supplying very acceptable 'natural' speech. The good people of Ipswich served long, and sometimes painful, hours as volunteer experimental subjects. Numerous individuals in the Human Factors Divison, the Speech Technology Division, and at BTRL generally, helped the programme of work along. We are very grateful to all these people. The responsibility for any errors or omissions, however, rests with the authors. Since finishing the text for this book, Mike Talbot has left British Telecom to join the National Health Service working with speech-impaired patients. I would like to express my thanks to him for his help over the last couple of years.

Acknowledgement is made to the Director of Research, British Telecom Research Laboratories, for permission to publish all chapters.

John Waterworth
Martlesham Heath, Suffolk
August, 1987.

1

Introduction

1.1. THE ORIGINS OF THIS BOOK

The work described in this book was carried out over the last three years, as part of an ongoing programme of designing, evaluating and improving a variety of predominantly speech-based systems. Each of these systems incorporated some combination of automatic speech recognition, speech synthesis, natural language processing, or intelligent dialogue control. More than any other branch of information technology, work on speech-based systems seems to pull together a wide and diverse range of disciplines. The intention of the book is to give a flavour for some of the main issues that were encountered during the period of work concerned, whilst considering how each of the disciplines contributed to their identification and solution.

The material in the following chapters is based on principles that have been drawn from the areas of cognitive psychology, ergonomics, linguistics, artificial intelligence, and cognitive science. The flavour of much of the work would suggest in fact that the barriers drawn amongst these disciplines are unnecessary, or at least inappropriate. A considerable amount of empirical testing and evaluation is reported, and this indicates our belief that the most important part of designing speech-based systems to be used *by* people has to involve testing their prototypes *on* people. There is still much to be learned about how humans produce and comprehend speech. It is only through finding ways of observing the processes more accurately that we will reach a stage where we can build computer-based systems that truly emulate those processes.

There is also considerable reference to existing, working speech-based systems. As well as recognising the importance of fundamental research into human speech and language processing, we believe that much can be learned from attempts to build working systems. Discussion is made of this in Chapter 2, but it deserves a mention here to give an idea of the emphasis of the book. The 'Sufficiency Principle' applies (Norman, 1980): theories of human speech processing need to be tested and evaluated. Working speech-based systems can be built which incorporate principles derived from such theories. If the systems carry out the speech processing with a similar success to that of the humans they seek to emulate, then the principles on which they are built constitute a sufficient explanation of those processes. Thus, products need to be developed on the basis of good theory, and their success or failure actually serves to evaluate that theory.

We hope we have struck a balance between our discussion of the applications of speech-based systems, and the theory upon which they are based. It is true to say that most of the work here would not have taken place had it not been for the purpose of developing working systems. But much of the material relates to systems yet to be fully implemented, and the book therefore gives an insight into the research being carried out today, to provide the basis for designing tomorrow's interactive services.

All of our work is founded on the belief that future systems must be more usable, in more natural and congenial ways, than traditional computer systems, and without extensive training. Our ultimate aim is 'Conversational Systems' with which one can discuss problems, obtain information and explanation, cooperatively solve problems, and obtain access to other systems and services as required. All of the work described relates to interaction via spoken or written language.

We have left out of this book a lot more material than we have put in. There is, for example, much more to be said about our work on discourse. This is essentially that part of the work which concerns the analysis of units larger than a sentence or clause, and which contributes to our understanding of the *structure* of conversation. This is likely to be a major focus for our research in the immediate future. There is also more to be said about our work on evaluating the quality of synthetic speech, specifically on evaluating the fidelity of its intonation contours. This is clearly also related to discourse, as it is largely the information content and the role of an utterance within a conversation that determines intonational aspects of the way it is spoken.

1.2. THE CHAPTERS IN BRIEF

Chapter 2 considers the ways in which the development of speech-based Information Technology (IT) has been influenced by psychology, and also how implementations of IT have affected psychological theories of speech perception. Some of the current problems associated with speech input and output devices can be attributed to the lack of attention their designers have paid to the processes of human speech production and perception, and this deficit is described. For example, with text-to-speech synthesis systems, little attention has been paid to the way in which humans use stress and intonation to indicate the information content and discourse role of utterances. This has resulted in the rather monotonous, uninformative drawl that characterises many speech synthesisers. Also, the most prevalent method for automatic speech recognition is based on a system that bears little or no relation to what is known about how humans recognise and understand speech. Some projects of the 1970s are then discussed, which were exceptional in that they tried to emulate the way in which the human speech understanding process was thought to work. They were thus characterised by the use of interacting sources of knowledge about the acoustics, syntax and semantics of language. These attempts were informed by theories of speech perception, but their results also allowed an appraisal of the validity of those theories.

In the third chapter, the emphasis shifts away from the theoretical bases of speech technology towards the products and their applications. This begins with a discussion of how the technology is being used in everyday situations. The benefits and the pitfalls of using this technology are discussed, and this leads on to a discussion of the performance levels of typical speech recognisers and synthesisers. What is observed is that, not only are the performance levels lower than is generally expected, but also there is a problem with the credibility of how these levels are measured. Different types and makes of system cannot be accurately compared using existing metrics, which are often misleading and ill-defined. Some alternative performance metrics are proposed.

In the light of the inadequacy of the performance scales discussed in Chapter 3, the next chapter reports some work that was aimed at establishing a suitable metric for the intelligibility of synthetic speech. The requirements for such a metric are firstly outlined. These are that it should be a valid indicator of the intelligibility of speech, and not of some other artefact; that it should be reliable, in that it always produces similar results under similar conditions; and that it should also take account of what is known about the process of human speech perception. The work goes on to propose one such metric. The results of the metric's successful evaluation are then reported. What is arrived at is a single index of intelligibility based on the time listeners take to recognise words spoken in synthetic speech. This satisfies the initial criteria, as defined, and also takes account of how speech quality interacts with the level of meaning of the material being spoken.

Chapter 5 moves away from the considerations of synthetic speech, and concentrates on methods for improving the performance of simple speech recognisers. The premise of the chapter is that there is a fundamental mismatch between the characteristics of human speech, and the characteristics that are required by a typical speech recogniser for recognition to be accurate. The chapter reports an evaluation of some methods by which this mismatch is hoped to be resolved. What comes to light is that, if the stored voice templates are collected in a more friendly manner, this can affect users' voice patterns to such an extent that recognition will improve. There are also some interesting results from the reported attempts to make the recognition system adapt to the continuous changes in the user's voice. This has been shown to be possible when the adaptation is triggered externally, but the self-adaptive speech recognition system has not yet been attained. This has interesting consequences for other types of adaptive systems.

Having considered some problems and issues with the actual technology of speech-based systems, the emphasis then shifts to a different consideration: assuming an effective means of producing and understanding speech, what else do we need to produce a truly conversational computer ?

Chapter 6 tackles the issue of providing the computerised system with some representation of the interaction it is to have with its users. In a simple system, such as one intended for database queries, this is fairly trivial. The system asks the user a series of questions, with the intention of finding out which part of the database the user wants to know about. Thus, the interaction is represented within the system in terms of a number of variables or 'slots', the value of which needs to be known for the query to be answered. Each question that the system asks, then, is directed towards the instantiation of one or more of these variables. In more sophisticated systems, however, the various questions and statements that the system uses are likely to have less well-defined meanings or intentions. The meaning of each utterance will depend on the context in which it is used, and its particular role in the discourse. The problem, then, is how to encode these various meanings and their dependencies. This chapter discusses various solutions to this problem. Specifically, it proposes how utterances might be encoded in terms of what they intend to achieve in the discourse; it reviews a range of techniques for representing the dialogue and the background knowledge required to conduct it; and it discusses the benefits of having a dialogue controller which conducts the interaction between the user and the machine, whilst residing separately from the application software.

The penultimate chapter (7) considers the problem of how to make systems that will cope with natural language requests. The problem of natural language processing is to try and derive the meaning of what a user says (or types), given that there are a very great number of ways he or she might say the same thing, and also that in different contexts, they might use the same words to mean a completely different thing. This chapter prvides a brief summary of fairly simple methods that have been used for interpreting such natural language requests. It then gives some examples of applications for this type of method: for understanding and possibly summarising texts, for natural language interfaces to such things as database query systems, for text editing, and of course, for purely speech-based interactive systems. Taking a case study, the last part of this chapter reports an approach to designing a quasi-natural language interface to a speech-based system. This describes the technique of conversational analysis, by which the principles of naturally-occurring conversations are identified, formalised, and incorporated into the computerised system.

The final chapter concludes the book with a consideration of the lessons we have learned about the field to date, and some speculation on the prospects for the future.

2

The Psychology and Technology of Speech:

A Symbiotic Relationship ?

J. A. Waterworth

2.1. INTRODUCTION

Interaction with machines, by speech, is becoming increasingly common in a range of situations including consumer products, office systems, and for various general- and special-purpose telecommunications applications (Waterworth, 1984). Because text-to-speech synthesis is so flexible, it is increasingly being used as a means of presenting information to users of advanced computerised systems. Applications include voice output for a range of interactive information services, database enquiry, and electronic mail interrogation. Similarly, word-based speech recognition technology has begun to make an impact in the market place, although within a relatively restricted range of applications. This chapter discusses the role of psychology in the development and use of speech-based information technology (IT) and, to a lesser extent, the relationship of IT implementations to psychological theories of how humans process speech. The ephemeral nature of speech, and the complex relationship between people and the spoken word, means that the success of technology incorporating speech is particularly dependent on psychological factors such as listeners' cognitive processing characteristics and how these interact with the medium.

The technology of speech attempts, to varying levels of detail, to duplicate human capacities for speech interpretation and production. As yet, however, all such implementations fall short of realising this aim fully. The limitations of the technology emphasise the need for sound psychological research to maximise the effectiveness of systems at their current level of development.

In discussing speech generation, particular emphasis is placed on the problems of using synthetic speech as a means of transferring information from systems to their users. The way in which automatic text-to- speech synthesis has been approached is described, and related to human speech production. Studies of human processing of synthetic speech are then reviewed, and some conclusions drawn.

Speech recognition or, more ambitiously, speech understanding has proved a much more intractable problem both technically and theoretically, and has had a larger impact on psychological theory than is the case with synthesis. Some of these theoretical aspects are reviewed in the second part of the chapter, which is divided into two sections. In the first, relevant psychological issues in human speech perception are reviewed. The second focusses on attempts to achieve automatic speech recognition, and how these relate to the underlying theoretical issues.

Recent advances in what is technically feasible have also led to a shift in psychological approaches to cognition in general, and speech processing in particular. The relationship between the two areas could thus be characterised as a symbiotic one.

2.2. SPEECH PRODUCTION

2.2.1. Text-to-Speech Synthesis

The impact of psychological theory on the development of speech IT products is evident in the design of text-to-speech synthesis devices. These machines, which can take most ordinary text (in electronic form) and convert it to and understandable speech output, are becoming increasingly prevalent. They have the obvious advantage, over earlier stored-waveform devices, of flexibility.

Devices that depend on storing human speech in some form are clearly limited to the vocabulary elements available (although some flexibility is achieved by novel concatenations of these elements), and bear little or no relation to the way humans produce speech. Text-to-speech synthesisers are built around simplified conceptions of human speech production of the sort illustrated in Figure 2.1. This architecture will be used to outline some of the background issues relevant to speech production in machines and humans.

Allen (1980) describes the sequence of events involved in text-to-

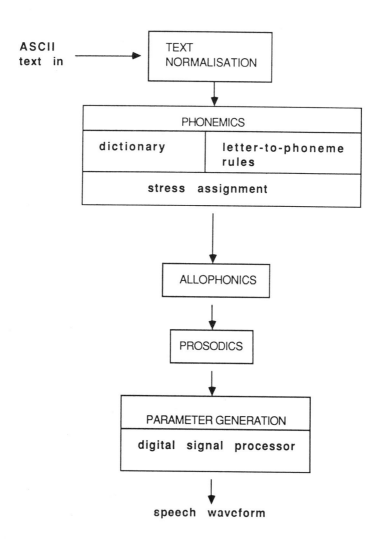

Figure 2.1 - Typical Text-to-Speech Architecture

speech conversion, which he claims "seeks to mirror the human cognitive capability for reading aloud" (p 388). The text is first 'normalised' (see Figure 2.1) to convert all tokens in the text into full alphabetic forms; 'Mr' will be converted to 'mister', and '11th' to 'eleventh', for example. At the next stage, phonemic analysis, an attempt is made to match words and parts of words (prefixes, suffixes, and roots) to a dictionary of 'morphs' (letter versions of morphemes).

In this way, exceptionally spelled high-frequency words are identified, as are the component morphs of a large number of multi-morphic words, including novel combinations of these elements. Allen suggests that as much as 95% of words from randomly selected text can be successfully identified in this way, using a dictionary of 12,000 morphs. It should be noted that commercially available text-to-speech devices typically incorporate a dictionary of around three or four thousand morphs. The 'exceptions dictionary' is a look-up table that is used to identify the pronunciation of known words and parts of words.

Psychological studies of morphology (cited by Morton, 1981) support the idea that human language processing involves analysis in terms of morphemes. Murrell and Morton (1974) demonstrated that priming with a morphemically similar word (e.g. SEEN) facilitated later recognition of a target word (SEES), whereas a word that was physically, but not morphologically, similar (SEED) did not. Using the Lexical Decision Task, whereby subjects have to decide whether a string of letters is a word or not, Taft and Forster (1975) found that the presence of a morpheme within a letter string increased the time needed for the string to be rejected as a non-word, as compared to letter strings with no underlying morphemic content. Thus, the time to reject BESIST was significantly greater than that needed to reject BESCUE, presumably because -SIST is a psychologically-real morpheme, whereas -SCUE is not.

2.2.1.1. Table look-up versus computation

When a given input word (from the text) is not fully identified from entries in the exceptions dictionary, letter-to-phoneme rules are used to obtain the pronunciation of remaining letters or strings of letters. The rules for consonant conversion are relatively straightforward and are applied first. To arrive at vowel pronunciations, the surrounding phoneme context, as well as the individual letter, is taken into account in the rules. The success of the resulting speech output is obviously dependent on the adequacy of these letter-to-phoneme rules, at least for forms not present in the exceptions dictionary. A balance must clearly be drawn between the size of the dictionary and the number and/or complexity of the pronunciation rules. In commercial text-to-speech devices about 5000 rules will be implemented. In combination with an exceptions dictionary of around 3000 items, this allows most not-very-uncommon and not-too-irregular words to be pronounced adequately for most purposes.

The question of the balance of emphasis between table look-up and rule-based computation is a fundamental one in assessing attempts to model human cognitive functioning. Table look-up is fast and computationally inexpensive, but is very demanding in terms of storage requirements; rule-based approaches are efficient in terms of memory, but computationally demanding and hence, at least in serial processing implementations, slow. How this equation is balanced in human speech processing has been given more attention in relation to attempts to recognise human speech, than in the development of speech synthesis (see below). But it should be noted here that, in recent years, the idea that humans place a relatively heavier emphasis on table look-up, as against computation, than was previously thought, has been gaining credibility (e.g. Norman, 1980). The practical effect of this trade-off between rule-based computation and table look-up in text-to-speech devices, which are necessarily limited in both memory and computational resources, is a compromise between good pronunciation of common names and of parts of words present in the dictionary but poor pronunciation of words that are not catered for (the table look-up emphasis), and good pronunciation of most words that are not very irregularly spelled but with inadequate coverage of exceptions, some of which could be fairly common (rule-to-phoneme emphasis).

Stress assignment in current text-to-speech conversion is inadequate. When a word is identified by reference to the dictionary the main word stress is placed on the leftmost root, unless a suffix which itself attracts stress is present. Words subjected to letter-to-phoneme rules are subjected to fairly complicated, but not comprehensive, rules for stress placement derived from work such as that of Halle (e.g. Halle & Keyser, 1971). Again, in commercial implementations, the number of rules from which a stress assignment is derived is limited by cost considerations. A major source of inadequacy is the fact that stress assignment is not carried out on the basis of a syntactic parse of input sentences. This means that, although the stress on individual words spoken in isolation (in a list, for example) may be adequately specified, that of complete sentences is very restricted, resulting in stylised and unnatural stress placement.

At the next processing level, phonological rules are used to decide which allophonic forms are appropriate for each input sentence. The same phoneme can be produced in a variety of ways depending on context, and allophones are these alternative versions, found in actual speech, of particular phonemes. It is believed that native speakers

possess a finite set of such rules and apply them, largely uncons-
ciously, when producing or recognising speech (Dilts, 1984). Thus, it
takes a certain amount of conscious effort for English speakers to distinguish between the two allophones of the phoneme /t/ in 'top' and
'stop'. Without such effort, they are perceived as identical. In practice, not all of these phonological rules are known and, of those that
are, only a subset are implemented in current text-to-speech devices.

2.2.1.2. Prosody

The prosodic structure of an utterance covers such features as
intonation contours, timing, and stress. Intonation contours are typically assigned on the basis of a very crude sentential parse. Because
automatic text parsers are currently both unreliable and computationally expensive (Dilts, 1984), parsing is generally restricted to identifying major boundaries; in a commercial system this may be done
purely on the basis of punctuation. Allen's (1980) research implementation also identifies some parts of speech, on the basis of suffix and
prefix information, then carries out a left-to-right scan, with no back-
tracking, to spot nouns, prepositions, and verb phrases.

A major weakness with available text-to-speech schemes is the restricted intonational repertoire. Most devices cater for 3 or 4 'tunes'
covering two sorts of questions, and one or two sorts of statements.
This fact accounts for the tedious repetitiveness experienced when
listening to more than a few sentences produced by a particular synthesis device. And, as Silverman (1985) points out, not only are there
not enough 'tunes' available; they are often phonetically incorrect.
Silverman suggests that this accounts for the characteristic, and generally unpleasant, 'computer accent' of most synthetic speech. The
cues to phonemic identity that are believed to be carried in part by
pitch changes are either absent, ambiguous, or wrong in current synthesisers, and this has been suggested as one reason why listeners use
more effort to process synthetic than natural speech. Sorensen and
Cooper (1980) detail the complexities of intonation in human speech
production, which reflect syntactic form, but are largely absent from
current synthesis devices. This knowledge source also has a potential
role in speech recognition.

At another level, current synthesisers also fail to mimic the way
humans use speech prosody to signal informational structure (e.g. to
show that, "I have finished talking about one topic and am now moving on to another", or to signal that, "I am now coming to the important part") and dialogue role (e.g. to indicate when turntaking is to
take place; Beattie et al., 1982). This, and the very limited application
of intonational knowledge to speech recognition, reflect the way in
which speech production and recognition tend to have been

approached, as IT products have developed, as discrete processes; and a discrete speech synthesiser or recogniser knows nothing about informational context or communicative function.

Text-to-speech synthesis is too much of a passive, mechanical activity. Text is automatically converted to speech independently of meaning and, to a large extent, grammar. It is hardly surprising that such speech is perceived as unpleasant, unnatural, and repetitive, even when it is acceptably intelligible. Work is currently in progress to derive better rules for problematic aspects such as intonational structure (e.g. Silverman, 1985) and segmental durations (e.g. Klatt, 1980). At the higher level, this can only begin to make an impact in the context of interactive systems, in which knowledge of discourse topic, and conversational function, can be represented and brought to bear during speech production. The implication is, of course, that human speakers and hearers use such information in life, whenever it is available. A pioneering attempt to use topic knowledge in the process of synthesising speech is the 'Speech Synthesis from Concept' approach of Fallside and Young (e.g. 1984), which they applied to messages from a data-base containing water network information. This works by identifying the concept contained in an information request and interpreting the meaning of the request from what the system knows about the water network. This semantic representation is used as the basis for constructing output messages (via syntactic and phonological processes). Such an approach lends itself readily to the production of sophisticated prosodic forms on the basis of the meaning of what is being said.

2.2.2. Human Processing of Machine Speech

As machine speech has begun to achieve levels of intelligibility that are comparable to those obtained with natural speech, interest has focussed on psychological reasons for the fact that listeners continue to find synthetic speech harder to listen to and remember than natural speech. This attention has led to the revival of well-known psychological techniques for assessing memory performance, with comparisons being made between human and machine productions of the same experimental material. Several experiments have demonstrated poorer recall and comprehension of synthetic speech compared to natural speech.

2.2.2.1. Serially-ordered recall of word lists

Luce et al. (1983) carried out a study investigating the nature of the difficulty in retaining information presented synthetically, using ordered recall of 10-word lists. They found that it was the first few words of the list for which recall was most reduced by the use of synthetic as compared to natural speech; that is, there was a differential primacy effect. They suggested that this could result from differences in the cognitive effort required to encode and/or rehearse synthetic and natural speech. 'Rehearsal' here refers to hypothesised subjective strategies for maintaining items in short-term (i.e. 'working') memory that may, or may not, also result in the transfer of material to long-term memory. This difference in processing effort would lead to less cognitive capacity being available for constructing memory representations of synthesised speech than is available for natural speech, and hence there would be reduced ability to rehearse and store words for later recall. They point to a similarity to the problems encountered with noise-degraded speech, where it seems that difficulties in encoding produce difficulties in short-term memory and in subsequent recall from long-term store (e.g. Dallett, 1964; Rabbitt, 1966, 1968). This is compatible with a differential primacy effect since the primacy portion of the curve (items presented at the beginning of the list) is regarded as reflecting recall of material that has been transferred from short-term to long-term store.

Waterworth and Thomas (1985) carried out two experiments to identify the source of the synthetic speech deficit a little more precisely; that is, whether it is due primarily to encoding or rehearsal. Their first experiment was very similar to that of Luce et al. (1983), and compared recall of 10-word lists for natural and synthetic speech. They also found poorer recall for the synthetic lists, but here it was the recency, rather than the primacy portion of the curve which was differentially affected.

Their second experiment looked at the extent to which apparent recall deficits were in fact due to encoding difficulties, by measuring the extent to which misperceptions occurred. They asked some subjects to repeat each stimulus word as they heard it, and then corrected the recall scores by taking account of the number of items successfully repeated. In this case, the differences between the pattern of recall for the two types of speech were very small and not statistically significant. This result suggests that, at least for the experimental task used, the memory deficit with synthetic speech is mainly due to difficulties at the encoding stage.

The fact that in Luce et al.'s (1983) experiment it was the primacy portion of the curve which was differentially depressed with synthetic speech, whereas Waterworth and Thomas found the recency portion to be affected, would suggest the use of rather different strategies by the two sets of subjects. It seems that Waterworth and Thomas's subjects sacrificed the encoding of later items, so that earlier items could be maintained in memory, whereas Luce et al.'s subjects sacrificed the maintenance of earlier items to ensure accurate encoding of later items. Thus it appears that, when processing incoming synthetic speech, there is some flexibility in the allocation of short-term memory resources between the encoding of stimuli and rehearsal in memory.

2.2.2.2. Types of memory task

The studies discussed so far all looked at one task: that of recalling a list of words of known length in the presented order. Since different tasks place different demands on memory and may thus tap different memory strategies, it is of interest to know what happens when subjects perform different memory tasks. The serially-ordered list recall paradigm is also very artificial, compared to the situations in which listeners are likely to encounter synthetic speech output, which again supports the idea of examining performance on a range of tasks.

One way in which different task demands might affect memory performance is in the type of retention strategy a particular type of task encourages. Craik and Lockhart (1972) drew a distinction between two types of rehearsal strategy; maintenance and elaborative. They suggested that long-term retention is more dependent on the qualitative nature of the rehearsal than on sheer quantity. Maintenance rehearsal is characterised as simple repetition of items which serves to maintain some of those items within the cognitive system and postpones forgetting for as long as it continues, but without having any beneficial effects on a delayed recall task. Elaborative rehearsal, on the other hand, involves organization, image formation or use of some other mnemonic, and so would be expected to be beneficial for later memory performance due to the involvement of stimulus processing at a deeper level. Hanley and Thomas (1984) point to experimental evidence (Watkins & Watkins, 1974; Shallice, 1975) that in a serially-ordered memory task involving lists of words, subjects tend to adopt a specific memory process. If aware of list length, for example, they will tend to switch from elaborative to maintenance rehearsal as the end of the list approaches.

These observations led to a further experiment carried out by Furner (reported as Experiment 3; Waterworth, 1985) in which an experimental procedure similar to that of Waterworth and Thomas was used, with one major difference: a running memory task instead of serially-ordered recall was used. The running memory task involves presenting a list of items to the subject one at a time, and then at some point (unknown to the subject) the subject is stopped and asked to write down the last few presented items (a specified number, the value of which depends on the memory load being given to the subject) in the correct order. This means that the subject must lose items as well as take in new items for storage, and hence may well adopt a different approach to item memorisation. Using this procedure, Furner obtained results similar to those of Waterworth and Thomas. There was a differential recency effect between the two speech types, which disappeared on correction for encoding. Thus, it appears that for both the memorisation tasks used in these two studies, the significant problem was with encoding per se rather than with maintenance of encoded items in memory.

2.2.2.3. Sentences versus word lists

Results from experiments involving the memorisation of lists of unrelated words are, arguably, very artificial in character. It is also quite possible that different strategies are used with larger language units, such as sentences. Pisoni and Hunnicut (1980) compared recognition of meaningful and syntactically correct but meaningless ('anomalous') sentences, with natural and synthetic utterances. They found that, whereas recognition for meaningful sentences was 6% lower when they were presented in synthetic rather than natural speech, it was 19% lower for the meaningless sentences. They pointed out that listeners can recognise the words in meaningful sentences correctly by using several sources of knowledge available; morphology, syntax and semantics. However, in the meaningless sentences there was little more than the detailed analysis of the acoustic-phonetic information in the waveform available.

This result is not surprising, and replicates the classic finding that listeners use context to help them understand speech. Miller et al. (1951) presented words to subjects in noise, either as isolated single words, or within the context of a sentence. Context improved recall. In a more subtle demonstration of this effect, Miller and Isard (1963) used sentences with different levels of syntactic and semantic context. Using a recognition-in-noise task, they presented their subjects with three types of sentence: normal syntax and meaningful; normal syntax but meaningless; and ungrammatical and meaningless. Recognition rates were 89%, 79%, and 56%, respectively, demonstrating the facilitatory effect of syntactic and semantic context on word recognition. According to Pisoni and Hunnicutt (1980), the intelligibility and comprehension of meaningful synthetic speech sentences suffers relatively little compared to natural speech controls. However, with meaningless sentences (or isolated words), context cannot be used, so it is necessary to rely more on the acoustic-phonetic signal itself. As this is less than optimally specified with synthetic speech, significant deficits relative to natural speech are observed.

Using sentences instead of word lists might be expected to favour more elaborative strategies of rehearsal than those used with word lists. Another way of altering rehearsal strategy is to use different types of delay before recall. Mazuryk and Lockhart (1974) compared the effects of maintenance (overt repetition) and elaborative (generation of an associate) rehearsal on immediate and delayed recall of short lists containing five words. They found that elaborative rehearsal led to better delayed recall, but that on the immediate test the maintenance group were superior. They also found that a group allowed to rehearse five-word lists silently performed in virtually the same way as the maintenance group. This suggests that, given the choice, subjects simply repeat items when they know that the order to recall is imminent, and so if subjects are forced to delay for a short period before they can write down the sentence, they would presumably use this strategy.

A study by Waterworth and Holmes (1986) examined the nature of the synthetic speech deficit when testing recall of sentences, and how this compared to results obtained with word lists. The use of sentences, rather than of word lists, also allowed the influence of some contextual factors to be examined. A further point of interest was to look at what happens under conditions of delay, either an empty delay or a delay when the subject has another task to do. The experiment consisted of using meaningful and nonsense sentences under conditions of immediate recall, recall after an empty delay, and recall after a filled delay. The idea of testing nonsense sentences under immediate recall was that this provided a condition similar to that used by Waterworth and Thomas (1985), except that sentence structure was used instead of just a word list. The inclusion of this condition was to give an idea of the extent to which the results were being affected by the syntax of sentences (without meaning) as compared to earlier results with word lists. By comparing this condition with the meaningful sentences condition, additional effects of meaning could be assessed. Effects of delaying recall were examined by comparing the delay conditions with the immediate recall condition.

Certain results were expected from the experiment. Firstly, natural sentences would be recalled better than synthetic, and meaningful better than nonsense. Secondly, the use of nonsense rather than meaningful sentences would lead to a greater reduction in recall for synthetic speech than for natural speech (comparable to the findings of Pisoni and Hunnicutt, 1980). Thirdly, the use of sentences rather than word lists could lead to an altered pattern of results due to the use of a different memory strategy. It was also hoped that information would be obtained about the way rehearsal strategy affected recall and how cognitive capacity was allocated when remembering sentences, as follows. By presenting both meaningful and nonsense sentences under conditions of immediate recall and recall after an unfilled or filled delay, the absolute amount of rehearsal and the relative amounts of maintenance and elaborative rehearsal would be altered. More elaborative rehearsal would tend to be used with meaningful sentences, and with an empty delay subjects might be using both types of rehearsal. A filled delay, with the task of counting backwards in threes, would be expected to affect the two types of rehearsal to different extents; maintenance rehearsal would be blocked, but some elaborative rehearsal might still be possible.

The results obtained showed that although in general sentences in natural speech were recalled significantly better than those in synthetic speech, the fact that sentences were used, rather than word lists, greatly altered the pattern of recall across serial positions. The nonsense sentences with immediate recall condition was the most similar to the experiment on word lists by Waterworth and Thomas (1985), except for the fact that words were presented within a sentence structure. As in their study, a three-way interaction between voice type, list half, and serial position, indicated a differential serial order effect between the two voices. Unlike their results, however, this seemed to arise mostly from the primacy, not the recency portion. The presence of grammatical structure, which is essentially the only difference between this condition and the list memorisation used by Waterworth and Thomas, seemed to have altered the way subjects approached the memorisation task.

Subjects may have been allocating a greater proportion of their processing resources towards encoding items in this experiment, at the expense of transferring early items to long-term store or maintaining them in working memory. One could speculate that sentence structure encouraged this tendency, because subjects attempted to encode the complete sentence to capitalise on its structure in memorisation.

The interaction between meaning and voice type was not significant. This means that synthetic speech sentences were not more affected by being nonsense than were sentences in natural speech, which contradicts the findings of Pisoni and Hunnicutt (1980). This seems surprising, in view of the fact that acoustic-phonetic cues would undoubtedly be poorer with the synthesised speech, so the greater reliance on these that the presentation of nonsense sentences would necessitate would be expected to have a more detrimental effect with synthetic than with natural speech. The difference between findings can perhaps be attributed to the different tasks the two experiments used; Pisoni and Hunnicutt's subjects did not have to memorise and recall sentences, merely repeat them correctly. The result shows that memory for synthetic speech sentences does not benefit from context any more than does that for natural.

Recall for the two voice types was not significantly different, with a filled delay. Taken together with the fact that there was a significant interaction between voice and delay type, this suggests that a filled delay has a greater effect on recall of natural than of synthetic speech sentences, reducing performance of both voice types to the same level after the first few items. On the assumption that the filled delay task would make maintenance rehearsal virtually impossible, while still permitting some elaborative rehearsal, this suggests that the synthetic speech recall deficit can be characterised as a differential impairment of maintenance rehearsal, caused by the allocation of more cognitive resources to encoding than is the case with natural speech. Presumably this emphasis on encoding has less impact on elaborative than on maintenance rehearsal. As there was no differential memory enhancement between the two voice types as a result of context, it seems that, with immediate and unfilled delay conditions, subjects predominantly adopted maintenance rehearsal, whether the material was meaningful or not. Conversely, with filled delays, subjects could not engage in maintenance rehearsal, whether or not the material had meaning.

2.2.3. Implications for the application of speech synthesis products

As the recall of synthetic speech items does not benefit more from context than does that of natural, we can expect more or less the same degree of deficit to occur with synthetic speech when lists are presented as when grammatical sentences comprise the material to be memorised. The use of sentences seems, from the Waterworth and Holmes study, to result in differentially poor recall of early items presented synthetically, whereas Waterworth and Thomas (1985) found that, with lists, the synthetic speech deficit was greater towards the end of the list. When maintenance rehearsal is prevented because listeners are engaged in another processing task, recall of synthetic speech is not significantly worse than that of natural. This is encouraging from the point of view of using synthetic speech to convey important messages to listeners who are already engaged in other activities, for example when delivering automated warning messages.

That the extent of the synthetic speech deficit is not different for lists than for sentences suggests that one possible explanation for this deficit, inadequate intonation specification, may be less significant than is generally thought, since this factor would be expected to affect sentences more than lists. In other words, although more life-like intonation will no doubt improve the acceptability of synthetic speech to listeners, it is unlikely to improve memory performance. This view is supported by a study by Waterworth (1983) which demonstrated that, with lists of concatenated digits, subjective preference for the machine-controlled speech was enhanced by the use of more natural intonation forms, but recall performance was not. In contrast, the insertion of longer pauses between subgroups of digits improved recall, but did not affect subjective preference. Thus, subjective acceptability, as indicated by preference ratings, and objective performance do not necessarily go together in the case of machine-generated speech.

Further evidence for the facilitatory effect of pauses, on recall of synthetic material, was reported by Nooteboom (1983). He found that recall of synthetically- spoken sentences was enhanced by the insertion of larger-than-natural, but grammatical, pauses, while that of naturally-spoken sentences was not. Presumably the exaggerated pauses allowed rehearsal effort with synthetic speech (which would normally be depressed because of encoding demands) to more closely approximate the level achieved with natural speech.

The fundamental problem with current speech synthesis is the inadequate specification of acoustic cues to phonetic segments. This results in more effort being allocated by listeners to encoding than is the case with natural speech. Because capacity is limited, this allocation of resources to encoding is at the expense of rehearsing previously-encoded items. It has been suggested that maintenance, but not elaborative, rehearsal is impaired in this way. One simple way of improving memory for synthetically-presented material, to compensate for this impairment (pending the development of improved text-to-speech implementations), would be to insert exaggerated pauses at syntactic boundary points in sentences, or between groups of a few items when presenting lists.

2.3. SPEECH RECOGNITION

2.3.1. Introduction

The problem of achieving speech recognition by machine has had a greater impact on psychological views of human speech perception, and vice versa, than is the case with synthesised speech. As a prominent speech researcher observed five years ago (Pisoni, 1981), "Although a very formidable task, research in the future will be focused more directly on the general problem of spoken language understanding. In my view, it is here that the greatest insights into language processing will be found in the next ten years" (p. 257). With synthesis, designers have been able to take advantage of the great adaptability in speech processing possessed by humans; adaptability which allows them to interpret a wide variety of speech realisations, both natural and unnatural. In attempting speech recognition, the variability inherent in human speech production works against simplistic solutions. However, both topics are, in the long run, addressing the same fundamental problems, so that knowledge gained in attempting speech recognition is beginning also to benefit approaches to synthesis, and some synthesis work, for example that which aims to model human articulatory effects, is informing work on recognition. Although outside the scope of this article, it is worth noting that a large amount of the work on human speech perception at the acoustic level would not have been possible without engineering research into speech synthesis devices. Ainsworth (1976) comments that, "It was only when such machines had been developed to a stage where they could be used to generate speech-like sounds for psychoacoustical experiments, that the acoustic cues which are employed in speech recognition were isolated" (p. 59).

The traffic between the psychology and the technology of speech recognition has been two-way. Initially, work looking at the way people might interpret spoken language preceded practical developments in machine recognition. As the availability of relatively cheap processing power increased, attention focussed on implementations of recognition techniques, with behavioural research continuing in parallel, and largely independently. Most recently, a more truly symbiotic relationship has developed between the two disciplines. This section briefly outlines some developments in both areas, taking a roughly historical perspective.

2.3.2. Human Speech Perception

2.3.2.1. The problem

How does a listener identify what a speaker is saying ? In other words, how are the sounds which reach the ear used to select, from the listener's mental lexicon, the words the speaker had in mind when producing the speech sounds ? This is, in very simplified form, the problem that theories of human speech perception attempt to account for, and which automatic speech recognition techniques attempt to solve. Closely related to this, of course, is the question of how a speaker's intentions are translated into the production of speech sounds.

Two main questions dominated early psychological work in the area: what is the 'minimal speech unit', and how do people cope with the lack of acoustic-phonetic invariance in speech ? The quest for a minimal speech unit is based on the idea that speech is represented centrally as a set of discrete entities into which incoming speech is decoded for the purposes of speech recognition, and from which speech is encoded during speech production. The main contenders for this role are the phoneme and the syllable.

A problem for any 'minimal unit' account of speech perception is the fact that there is no one-to-one correspondence between acoustic events in the speech signal and the phonetic information such events signify. One acoustic event may carry information about several neighbouring linguistic segments, and the way a segment is specified depends on surrounding events. This 'coarticulation' problem is a function of the speed with which vocalisation articulators (tongue, lips, throat, etc.) move during speech, which results in gestures towards target positions, rather than direct hits on specified vocal cavity configurations. How listeners are able to reconstruct, from speech productions, just what those targets were and, hence, what the intended phonetic information was, is an abiding mystery. Another problem is that of segmentation; the physical characteristics of the speech signal vary continuously, but the perception of speech is categorical. On what basis is the speech signal segmented into the discrete categories apparently needed for speech recognition ?

Liberman et al. (1967) were influential in popularising the phoneme as the main contender for the basic unit of speech perception. The phoneme has the advantage of parsimony; there are only about 40 phonemes in English, compared to over 1000 syllables and, of course, many more words. An attendant disadvantage, however, is the rate of processing this implies which, at around 12-15 identification decisions per second (assuming a serial processing architecture), is beyond the capacity of the human system (Miller, 1962); nor could articulators produce phonemes at this rate.

2.3.2.2. Motor Performance Hypotheses

The problems of continuity and variability of expression led Liberman et al. (1967) to develop their motor command hypothesis. By this account, the invariance necessary for speech communication lies at the level of 'phonemic intentions', as embodied in invariant and discrete commands to articulators. Through articulation, these commands are converted, by virtue of the inertia of the articulators and the speed of the neuro-muscular system, into variable and continuous acoustic output. By using this knowledge about how to produce speech in reverse, as it were, it is suggested that listeners are able to work out what the speaker's phonemic intentions were when producing a particular acoustic stream via the articulators. The listener does this, apparently, by running simulations of converting phonemic intentions into articulatory responses and testing the outcomes against the acoustic stream that is being received. As Henderson (1982) points out, this analysis-by-synthesis approach only treats segmentation at the level of these simulated acts, not at all at the acoustic level. Because articulatory expression can be influenced by the surrounding context, phonemic information can be said to be encoded in parallel in the speech stream, thus avoiding the limitations on both production and identification of phonemes implied by serial coding. Both speakers and hearers appear to be unaware of the knowledge it is suggested they are applying to produce and recognise speech. Liberman et al. (1967) suggested the existence of a special-purpose perceptual mechanism responsible for the analysis-by-synthesis process: the speech decoder.

The 'motor command' hypothesis of Liberman et al. (1967) has attracted a fair amount of criticism in recent years. MacNeilage (1970), for example, showed on the basis of EMG readings that the commands are not actually invariant. An alternative, based on the invariance of articulation targets rather than commands, the 'vocal tract target' hypothesis, was suggested (MacNeilage & MacNeilage, 1973). Both approaches suffer from the fact that information about the physical production of speech is needed to make sense of incoming speech. Of just what this information is comprised is largely unknown (consciously) to speakers and hearers. Researchers are limited by the methods available to acquire such physiological information, which tend to be difficult and, currently, very time consuming. Other arguments against motor theories of speech perception include the fact that some individuals who have always been incapable of speaking nevertheless have excellent speech comprehension abilities (Fourcin and Lennenberg, 1973), and that discrimination of intonation contours is as good in non-speakers as in normals, whereas intonation by deaf individuals is usually much degraded from normal (Fourcin, 1975).

From the standpoint of psychology, one could argue with Morton (1981) that there is no dependent relationship between psychological and physiological descriptions. According to him, "there is no piece of physiological or anatomical data that could verify or falsify a purely psychological model" (p. 389). In terms of psychological theory, strictly defined, what happens below the level of cognition is irrelevant. But from the point of view of speech science, anything that can be brought to bear on the speech problem is valid, and probably necessary for an adequate understanding of verbal behaviour.

Knowledge about human articulation of speech has not made much of an impact on approaches to automatic speech recognition as yet, although synthesis techniques that closely model human speech production are under development (e.g. Scully, 1984). One advantage of this approach is that synthesisers with individual and highly natural speaking styles could be produced, with obvious advantages for handicap-related applications. It is possible that the knowledge on which this type of synthesis-by-rule is based can be successfully used to overcome the problem of speaker dependency in speaker recognition, by generating recognition templates for particular speakers on the basis of an analysis of their articulatory characteristics (see, for example, Bridle and Ralls, 1985). A problem with such approaches, however, is the very high computational demands of modelling articulatory behaviour adequately. Currently, this cannot be done in real time.

2.3.2.3. The Role of Auditory Processing

A less radical approach than the abandonment of segmentation from acoustics is to suggest that direct segmentation of the incoming speech signal is possible, despite problems of continuity and variability of expression, if these segments are at a higher level than the phoneme. Several authors have suggested that the syllable may be the basic unit for lexical access, rather than the phoneme (e.g. Massaro, 1975; Mehler, 1981). Syllables are less variable in expression than phonemes (although there are many more of them), thus the invariance problem is less severe, and are less difficult to segment since they are more temporally separate than phonemes (the discreteness problem). This also applies to larger entities such as the word, the clause (Bever et al., 1969), and the sentence (Miller, 1962). Words are not separated by silence in natural speech, and so might be thought to be harder to identify, acoustically, than the larger units. Prosodic features carry information which could assist the detection of words and larger syntactic units, but their interpretation is not simple (see, for example; Bolinger, 1972; Cutler, 1977).

Despite these attacks, the old idea that phonemes are the fundamental unit of speech perception, and that they can be identified directly from incoming speech patterns, refuses to die. Cole and Scott (1974) refuted the motor command hypothesis by suggesting that phonemes are sufficiently invariant, and there is enough information in the acoustic signal, for phonemes to be identified directly. Evidence for this view is provided by a study by Cole et al. (1980). This describes how one of the authors, Victor Zue, was able to successfully identify 97% of phonetic sentences from spectrograms of both normal and nonsense sentences, following 2000 hours of training. Because spectrograms provide records of acoustic events only, the authors suggest that this shows that Liberman et al. (1967) were wrong on two counts: direct segmentation is possible, and a special-purpose speech decoding mechanism is not necessary for phoneme identification (since only a visual representation was available). Cole et al. (1980) believe that their findings show that "there exists a great deal more phonetic information in the speech signal than was previously believed, and that such information is often explicit and can be captured by rules" (p. 46). They go on to suggest that the significance of this for automatic speech recognition is that attention to improving the acoustic processing front-end of systems will bear dividends.

It is rather unlikely that any one of the 'minimal units' referred to above is necessarily or exclusively used in speech perception. The level of analysis is probably a function of the processing task faced by the listener. In an experimental situation, the task given to subjects will influence the aspects of the incoming signal that are the focus of attention, and hence the minimal unit identified. Thus we may be finding out more about strategies for coping with the task than about normal speech perception (Barry, 1984). Also, the phoneme may have an essential role in lexical access, but this does not necessarily mean that syllable or word level segmentation are not also used, nor that phonemes are identified in the speech flow at all.

From the discussion of research aimed at identifying the minimal unit of speech perception it might be concluded that the accepted view is that human speech processing normally relies on this process alone. This is not the case, despite the (possibly undue) interest the topic has aroused. In fact, as Cole and Jakimik (1980) point out, "It is an axiom of speech perception that listeners use context to understand speech." (p. 140). It is commonly accepted that knowledge at several levels can be brought to bear to help disambiguate the acoustic evidence; to select the one correct interpretation of what the speaker intended from the multitude of possible interpretations that could account for the acoustic data alone (e.g. Reddy, 1976).

The direct perception of phonemes, or of some other 'minimal unit', might be possible in some circumstances, but normally all sources of information that can be used will be used. This is the view of Reddy (1976) and of Marslen-Wilson and his co-workers (e.g. Marslen-Wilson, 1980; see below). In attempting speech 'perception' by machine, acceptance of this type of approach has led to the process being viewed as speech understanding rather than speech recognition. While commonly accepted, this is not the universal view, however. In recent years attention has swung back to the possibility of more direct perception of speech, not necessarily involving interaction between various hypothesised knowledge sources at 'run time'. This type of approach has arisen, interestingly enough, from relatively unsuccessful attempts to implement speech understanding systems that exhibit such interaction, as identified in human speech perception by psychologists such as Marslen-Wilson, though not necessarily adhering closely to any particular psychologically-motivated model. We return to this topic in the section on automatic speech recognition.

2.3.2.4. Marslen-Wilson's Model

On the basis of evidence from speech shadowing and word monitoring studies, Marslen-Wilson (1980) asserts that, because of the speed with which these operations can be carried out, spoken word recognition appears to be interactive in character. Reviewing several studies by himself and his co-workers, he concludes that, on both tasks, listeners had achieved word recognition "after little more than half the acoustic input corresponding to the words could have been heard" (p. 45). A similar interpretation was placed on the results of phoneme-monitoring studies (Morton & Long, 1976; Dell & Newman, 1978), and of gating tasks (Grosjean, 1979). Under the gating paradigm, successive 30 ms fragments of the speech signal for a word are revealed, until the listener is able to identify the word. When presented within normal sentences, listeners could do this at about half way into the word. Further support comes from mispronunciation detection studies, including his own investigations of speech shadowing behaviour (Marslen-Wilson, 1975). In the latter, listeners were much more likely to repeat back corrections of mispronounced words when they were in the context of a normal sentence, than when they were in a semantically anomalous sentence. Corrections were also more likely with words in semantically anomalous sentences than in semantically and syntactically anomalous sentences, or with words in isolation. The fact that words tended not to be corrected if the first syllable was mispronounced, but were very likely to be if the second or third syllable was, was taken to demonstrate that contextual and sensory information have reciprocal roles, but that the latter is initially given priority.

Marslen-Wilson (1980) suggests that, as acoustic and contextual knowledge interact in the process of word recognition, so do two aspects of contextual knowledge; structural (syntactic) and interpretive (semantic). Tyler and Marslen-Wilson (1977) tested the hypothesis that syntactic analysis is independent of interpretation by varying the interpretive contexts in which syntactically ambiguous sentences were analysed. They found that context had a profound effect on syntactic analysis, as assessed by measuring naming latencies. Marslen-Wilson concludes that the results show that, "on-line sentence processing involves the rapid and sophisticated integration of at least three different sources of information - lexical, structural, and interpretive. No single one of these sources of information could have been sufficient by itself to produce a preference" (p. 52).

In addition to interaction between knowledge sources, the model makes three important claims: optimal efficiency in the processing strategy adopted, bottom-up processing priority, and obligatory processing. Optimal efficiency means that an analysis is carried out in such a way that it can be achieved, with a reasonable degree of certainty, as early as this is possible. For a word, this will be at some point after the start of the word, when all other possible word candidates have been eliminated (the set of possible word candidates is referred to as the 'cohort'). Marslen-Wilson (1980) presents evidence in support of optimal processing, showing that words are identified as soon as is theoretically possible, given the structure of real English words. Unfortunately, this claim can only be tested practically for isolated words, although Marslen-Wilson assumes the principle applies to the speech procesing system in general. If this is the case then the system must be interactive in character, since information from various knowledge sources could eliminate members of the cohort as possible word candidates in a particular sentential context.

As regards the assignment of priority to information from various knowledge sources, i.e. the processing control structure, Marslen-Wilson (1980) concludes that bottom-up priority is obligatory, at least as regards normal, 'on-line', speech recognition, and that this allows the analysis to maintain close contact with the sensory input. "If higher-level knowledge sources are allowed too much influence, then speech understanding runs the risk of becoming a process of hallucination rather than of synthesis" (Marslen-Wilson, 1980, p. 60), a comment that could be appropriately applied to some of the more ambitious automatic speech understanding schemes of the ARPA project (see below). Direct top-down processing is thus not possible in normal speech recognition, so that possible word candidates are not eliminated in advance of sampling acoustic events. In other words, context can come into play in reaching a decision only once the initial cohort has been selected on the basis of acoustic analysis. Although the results of higher level analyses may not be required to eliminate all but one word candidate, it is nevertheless obligatory that they are carried out. This can still be optimally efficient if it is assumed that cohort processing is distributed, implying a parallel processing architecture. When multiple knowledge sources are needed their analyses are carried out interactively, but priority is always given to information from the lowest level by which a word can be identified.

2.3.3. Automatic Speech Recognition

2.3.3.1. Templates

The most widespread, and commercially available, approach to automatic speech recognition arguably bears, in its simplest form, no direct relation to psychological theories of speech perception whatsoever; this is whole-word template matching. The method involves obtaining one or more samples of one or more speakers producing every word that is to be recognised, and storing representations of these utterances via a 'vocoding' (filtering and digitising) process. This is known as 'training' the recogniser. When in recognition mode, samples are taken in essentially the same way, but rather than being stored each is compared against some or all of the stored templates. If the incoming sample matches one of the stored templates to a criterion goodness-of-fit, then the word has been recognised as the same as the stored template. 'Words' here can be actual words or short phrases. Early devices tended to be 'single word' recognisers, each sample having to be separated by a pause of a certain length. More recently, so-called 'connected speech' devices have appeared, which can accept longer input strings (again separated from each other by pauses) and compare several templates against all or part of the input.

This approach is not a serious contender as a model of human speech perception, as it relies on the assumption that speakers produce utterances by stringing together stored representations of words. This is, of course, "a speech pattern generation process that nobody would seriously contemplate as a model of human speech production (but it has been used successfully for speech synthesis)" (Bridle & Ralls, 1983, p. 3). This, and recognition based on template matching, suffer from the same problem; limited vocabulary. A whole-word template matching recogniser can only ever be successful on those words with which it has been trained. Nor can it succeed in the recognition of continuous, rather than connected word, speech; there are just too many comparisons to be made and no basis, not even pauses, to limit the identification and combination of elements considered.

With a reasonably large vocabulary, it is obviously inefficient to search the entire template set for a match to every incoming 'word' sample. If the likely candidates at each point can be restricted by taking into account what has gone before, then the chances of success are undoubtedly raised. This also brings us slightly closer to modelling human speech recognition, where syntactic knowledge is used to assist the elimination of unlikely word candidates, since a grammar can be seen as a set of rules for what comprises a legitimate sequence in a particular language. Grammars can be used to generate and decompose (or parse) natural languages, or application-related subsets of natural languages, and come in various degrees of complexity and power (Chomsky & Miller, 1963). Two important types for speech recognition purposes are "slot-and-frame" and "finite state" grammars (Lea, 1980, p. 51). Slot-and-frame syntax specifies what words are permissible fillers for slots in the larger context of a specified frame. A frame could comprise the sequences of commands needed to carry out a particular operation, with a set of alternatives at each of several stages (slots) in these sequences. This technique has been successfully used with both isolated and connected word devices, to restrict the number of alternative templates considered at each decision point.

2.3.3.2. Markov modelling

The performance of template matching devices has been greatly enhanced in recent years by the adoption of the Markov methodology, based on the application of finite state grammars. As the name suggests, finite state grammars specify what state, from a limited number of states, can follow what state. In terms of word sequences within a language, which words will be considered for recognition at each point depends on a fixed memory of the previous word or words recognised, and is determined by an analysis of the probabilities of particular word combinations. This is, however, an over-simple characterisation of natural English which, as Chomsky (1957) showed, cannot account for the full complexity of the language. But it can be successfully applied to recognition on a strictly limited subset of English. For this reason, the Markov approach is not extensible to the recognition of unrestricted speech, nor can it be said to model adequately the human capacity for using grammatical structures. Higher order, more powerful grammars, are needed to extend recognition capability beyond tightly restricted language applications.

The Markov approach has been very successfully applied to isolated and connected word recognition, to dramatically enhance performance of inexpensive, 'trained', and limited vocabulary systems. In this type of application, it is applied to the various pronunciations of each vocabulary word, as specified by a set of probabilities for the co-occurrence of a number of within-word states. Thus, a word is represented in computer memory as a table of probabilities of changes between states, rather than a vocoded version of the word sample obtained during training. To obtain the probability values for the co-occurrence of these sub-word acoustic events (states), several samples of each word are needed. The calculation of these probabilities comprises the training phase of this type of approach, and is computationally expensive. Once trained, however, incoming utterances can be compared against probability tables at relatively little computational cost, with obvious advantages in system response time. Systems based on this approach have been able to achieve at least the level of recognition delivered by earlier template matching devices, and at a fraction of the cost. Template matching requires computationally expensive processes such as 'dynamic time warping', which must be carried out during the recognition phase to cope with the variations in pronunciation of a word that Markov modelling deals with 'automatically', by precompilation. Computational requirements can be reduced to the level where no specialised hardware is needed at all (Moore, 1984). Cheaply available software implementations of this approach have led to a significant increase in the incorporation of speech recognition into relatively inexpensive IT products.

2.3.3.3. Multiple knowledge sources and alternative architectures

Word or, at best, phrase recognition of the type achieved by the processes outlined above, is clearly not an adequate model of human speech interpretation. Devices operating along these lines have serious weaknesses. They have to be 'trained' on speech samples from the individuals who are going to use them, and they have a strictly limited vocabulary of words that they can possibly recognise, unless they are retrained. It began to be suggested in the early 1970s that, to extend the possibilities of machine speech recognition beyond these constraints, multiple knowledge sources would have to be used by the machine. It was thought that taking account of multiple knowledge sources such as prosodic, syntactic, semantic, and pragmatic information would allow true machine speech understanding, since at that time the dominant view was that recognition, based only on acoustic information, is impossible with unconstrained speech. This conclusion stemmed from the limited usefulness and extensibility of simple matching schemes such as those outlined above, and from psychological evidence of the type reviewed in the previous section. The outcome was the initiation of several ambitious speech understanding projects, supported by the US Advanced Research Projects Agency (ARPA), as well as related work in human speech studies (e.g. Marslen-Wilson, 1980).

The knowledge sources that are considered useful, at least potentially, in assisting the process of speech interpretation can be seen as lying on a continuum of levels representing closeness to the speech signal itself. From the bottom up these include signal, parametric, segmental, phonetic, syllabic, lexical, phrasal, and conceptual levels, corresponding roughly to the hierarchy of knowledge sources illustrated in Figure.2.2 (adapted from Goodman & Reddy, 1980, p. 236). The crucial question, with a complex scheme such as this, is how do the levels interact in coming to a decision about a sample of speech ? The simple hierarchy in Figure 2.2 would suggest that speech understanding is completely data-driven, from the bottom up, so that the signal must be correctly analysed before significant features can be looked for, and this latter task must be successful before lexical selection can begin, which in turn must precede parsing of the input into syntactic classes leading, finally, to working out the meaning of the utterance. In other words, higher level information cannot correct earlier errors in interpretation, and while missing details might be restored at a higher level this is made more difficult because higher levels do not inform lower level analyses. The converse of this structure is the goal-directed model (Goodman & Reddy, 1980), where top-level information drives the analysis at successively lower levels, although the results of lower level analysis are reported back up. In general, this sort of linear interaction scheme is ineffective because of the error-prone nature of speech processing at each level, and the restriction the scheme places on which other information source can

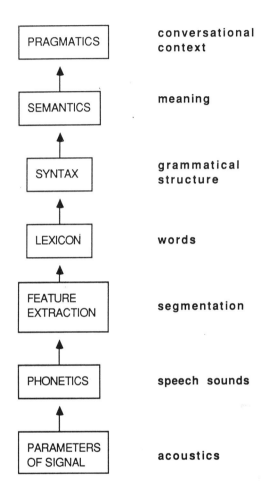

Figure 2.2 - Hierarchical Model of Speech Knowledge Sources

be called on to assist what process.

One way to avoid the limitations of linear interaction between levels of knowledge is to let every knowledge source interact with every other. The problem with such a 'heterarchical' scheme is that potential interactions become too complicated to handle, and each individual knowledge source must know how to interact with every other.

One of the more ambitious projects carried out under the ARPA initiative, HEARSAY-II, attempted to solve this problem by means of a 'blackboard' model of knowledge source interaction. This is illustrated in Figure 2.3 (adapted from Goodman & Reddy, 1980, p. 239). Under this scheme, according to Reddy (1980),
"Each knowledge source (KS) is viewed as an information gathering process which places ('writes') all its hypotheses on a globally accessible 'blackboard'. These hypotheses can then be used by other KSs to validate and/or reject an hypothesis and to create new hypotheses at other symbolic levels" (p. 218). In HEARSAY-II, different sources of knowledge are autonomous parallel processes. This bears a close similarity to Marslen-Wilson's model of human speech perception, where multiple information sources are processed in parallel, and cooperatively. The main difference is that HEARSAY-II does not give priority to low-level information.

HEARSAY-II has been very influential as a model of human information processing in general, and of speech understanding in particular (see Rumelhart, 1977). It has also been extended further, for example to model cooperation between humans (rather than between knowledge sources) in the process of engineering design (Whitefield, 1984). Norman (1980) comments that HEARSAY-II fulfils his psychological intuitions about the form of a general cognitive processing structure, using high level knowledge to guide heavy parallel computation on information from multiple knowledge sources. But HEARSAY-II was less successful than the winning project, HARPY; and HARPY approaches the problem rather differently.

2.3.3.4. Harpy

Problems with the HEARSAY-II approach include focussing attention on the most important pieces of information coming in from multiple knowledge sources, how to limit the amount of information-gathering each source carries out, and the communication of knowledge between different parts of the system. HARPY simplifies things by compiling all knowledge sources into a single integrated network prior to run-time, and uses left-to-right constrained search that is segment- rather than event-driven. Parallel processing is limited to only the best few alternatives (Reddy, 1980). A crucial difference between HARPY and HEARSAY-II is the greater emphasis given to bottom-up information. The precompiled network represents a "complete description of every pronunciation of every possible sentence" that the system can recognise (Goodman & Reddy, 1980, p. 238). An input signal is transformed by moving up the hierarchy to arrive at segmented and phonetically labelled strings; the best path within the network represents what is recognised. This approach inspired and has been developed by Klatt as a means for identifying words directly

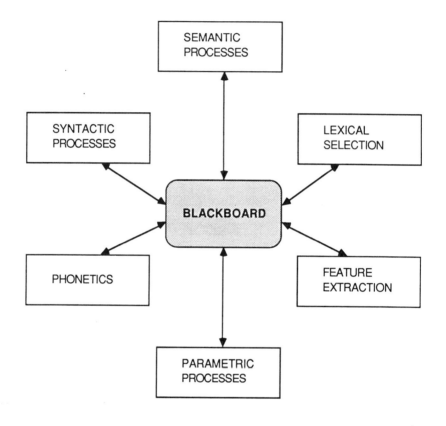

Figure 2.3 - Blackboard Model

from acoustic information, the LAFS (Lexical Access From Spectra) scheme (Klatt, 1980), which obviously has strong implications for speech perception research.

Norman (1980) finds himself impressed and depressed by the success of HARPY. He is impressed because, basically, it works; at least in terms of the target set by the ARPA initiative and, by this standard, it works better than HEARSAY-II (and the other projects carried out under the scheme). He is depressed because he finds HARPY implausible as a model of human speech understanding. He points out, as have others, that HARPY is inflexible. It depends for its success on prespecifying every pronunciation that can ever be recognised. It cannot take account of changes gathered from multiple sources of knowledge, and ignores higher-level knowledge. But the success of HARPY as a system, despite the limited nature of the test when compared to human performance with speech, has resulted in HARPY being taken very seriously as a model of human behaviour. Newell (1980), for example, claims that human cognition can be represented as a Production System, and goes on to demonstrate how HARPY can be modelled within this architecture.

The view that human cognition depends fundamentally on on-line computations, applied to a range of knowledge sources, is challenged by HARPY and replaced with the notion of storing the results of computations in memory, to be retrieved via some form of directed pattern matching. That is, HARPY suggests that humans put more emphasis on storing, retrieving, and matching patterns than was thought, and less on on-line computation. Rather than learning how to work out, from many sources of knowledge, what must have been spoken, language acquisition becomes a process of storing away vast numbers of patterns that represent all the possible pronunciations of all words an individual knows. The question of table look-up versus computation is also relevant in the context of speech synthesis (Waterworth & Holmes, 1986), and the same debate could be applied to human speech production. The issue has already begun to attract attention more generally, not only in Artificial Intelligence (e.g. Michie, 1980), but also in psychology (e.g. Broadbent et al., 1986). It is important to stress, however, that there is good reason to suppose that run-time processing on context (syntax, semantics, pragmatics) is carried out during speech processing, but the extent of this activity in normal speech perception and production is not currently known. The question is not whether table look-up or computation is used, but where the point of balance between the two lies for various cognitive tasks.

2.3.3.5. Associative models and interactive activation

The success of HARPY certainly resulted in a healthier regard for what can be extracted from the speech signal itself, emphasising processing from the bottom up, than had previously been the case. Perhaps even more importantly, it has also led to the belief that some intermediate levels of analysis, traditionally thought essential to achieve lexical access, may be unnecessary. The idea that we can store many versions of word pronunciations, and thereby move directly from speech signal to lexical access directly (and vice versa) is not new. Wickelgren (1969) proposed just such a scheme, whereby speech is represented in memory using associative coding, as underlying both perception and production. Sequences of speech events are represented by each event being specified in terms of the immediately preceding and following events. Wickelgren (1969) suggested overlapping triads of phonemes, so-called 'Wickelphones', although the nature of the coding is very uncertain. This sort of concept is highly applicable to distributed memory models based on interactive activation, whereby information is stored, at the neural level, not as discrete items that are in some way isomorphic with the information represented, but rather, "in the relationship among the [neural] units, and each unit participates in the encoding of many, many memories" (Hinton & Anderson, 1981, p. 3).

2.3.3.6. Conclusions

Such a view of memory, using context-sensitive, associative coding, implemented on highly parallel and distributed systems, is currently attracting considerable interest in several areas, including speech recognition. A recent paper by Marcus (1985) demonstrates the potential of associative models for dealing with the variability inherent in speech stimuli. It is probably fair to say that attempts to achieve human-like performance, by machine, on perceptual tasks such as this has led to the reinstatement of what was a largely discounted approach to human memory. In Artificial Intelligence, too, the idea of duplicating human performance at the neuronal level was popular in the 1960s, but was dropped because of the limited capacities of the machines at the time. With the development of relatively cheap, large, computer memories, the 'neural net' approach has been resurrected as a feasible model of human visual and auditory perception, and one that may overcome the limits in performance that other approaches seem to have reached. But, as already suggested, what is needed for speech recognition is not merely a large memory, but a "highly parallel, massively interactive processing system" (Elman & McClelland, 1985, p. 32). It remains to be seen how successful such approaches will be in practice. If they pass the test the implications for psychology, and for what is possible in the realm of Information Technology, will be enormous.

3

The Myth of Speech Technology

M. Talbot

3.1. INTRODUCTION

There is a certain mystique surrounding computers which can both produce and understand speech. This is because many people's impressions of speech technology have been coloured by the likes of HAL, the talking, listening computer in Arthur C. Clark's '2001'; by the speech capabilities of the BL 'Maestro' car (which announces low oil pressure, excessive temperatures, etc.), or by the antics of speaking dolls. That the applications of speech technology only impinge on people's lives in these very few and selective ways has meant that the true extent of its capabilities are generally not well known, and consequently the mystique is reinforced.

The truly conversational computer is much less a reality than is widely thought: although it was predicted a decade ago that speech input and output (I/O) devices would revolutionise the human-computer interface, allowing unrestricted, virtually error-free input and retrieval of data; possibly even automatic, speech-driven dictation of letters and documents, speech is still only being used in a few, select applications. Much of the reason for this is that the performance levels of speech I/O devices have not improved in accordance with predictions. However, it is also likely that certain groups who could benefit from using the technology are actually deterred from doing so by the fact that they do not know what it can offer them: scepticism is created by the distinct lack of objective and universal performance measures which exist for speech I/O devices.

I hope to dispel some of the myths of speech technology by considering three things:

(1)   What the technology can do, and how it is currently being put to work in the domain of human-machine interaction;

(2)   What typically quoted performance figures of speech synthesisers and speech recognisers are, and what is the worth of such figures;

(3)   How the performance levels of speech I/O devices should be assessed and described, such that their true capabilities are more meaningfully stated and thus made more accessible to a general user population.

I then want to make some projections regarding the course of likely developments in the area of speech I/O between now and the end of the century. However, I do not intend to provide either a comprehensive product guide, a detailed explanation of the workings of speech I/O devices, or a comparative evaluation of currently available speech products.

3.2. EXAMPLE APPLICATIONS OF SPEECH I/O

Many of the predictions that were made about the potential uses of speech technology concerned its application in the electronic office. However, that there are still very few such applications of speech I/O implies that such predictions were not well informed by practical considerations. The use of Automatic Speech Recognition (ASR) for recording and entering data to a computerised system, or of synthetic speech for output from a similar system, is ideal in situations where the operators' hands are full, and/or where their line of sight either must be directed away from the input device or is in some way impaired (Visick et al., 1984). Such situations seldom exist in office-based tasks. Not surprisingly, then, an extensive search of the available literature found few successful applications of speech I/O in the office, but many in the following settings:

(1)   In jobs in manufacturing and inspection;

(2)   For disabled people whose sight or mobility is impaired;

(3)   In aviation.

To achieve my first aim, of describing what speech technology can do, I will describe some sample applications of speech I/O, drawn from the above settings.

3.2.1. Industrial Applications

The common denominator amongst the successful applications of speech I/O in industry is that, in the job involved, it is inconvenient or time-consuming for the operator to keep moving to a device to enter some form of data. Thus, it is preferable to make the requisite entries simply by speaking them, rather than writing them down or entering them to a computer through a keyboard. For example, at the Ford factory in Cologne, Germany, ASR is currently in daily use for the recording of data regarding containers and packages leaving the warehouse (Rehsoft, 1984). This recording is performed by workers handling the (often large) packages in the despatch department, and is intended to keep a daily record of movements of deliveries out of the warehouse. The old system required manual input of the information carried on each package's invoice, such that the operators would have to put down the package prior to data entry; they were restricted in their movement, in that they could not leave the terminal area where data entry was performed; and new operators would require considerable training before they could operate the system efficiently. The use of ASR, with operators wearing wireless head microphones and radio transmitters, alleviated each of these restrictions. Its introduction allowed efficient data entry whilst physically handling loads, whilst moving around within the work area, and without operators having to undergo as much training. The implementors of the system achieved 98% recognition accuracy (that is, the percentage of words spoken which were correctly recognised by the system), and as a result of its introduction were able to do the same work with many less operators. ASR is being used in a similar fashion by General Electric in the USA. Details of incoming packages are entered by speech to the record system, but in this case, the operator is given feedback of her or his entry by way of a synthetic speech 'echo'.

Inspection lines also seem to have benefitted considerably from the introduction of ASR. In a similar way to the package handlers, the inspectors can work much more efficiently if they do not have to take their hands or eyes off the item under inspection. This applies equally to fine inspection of small items and to large-scale inspection. For example, the inspector may be using a microscope to inspect circuit boards and does not want to look up to make notes and then have to re-focus on the image. Or he or she may not want to let go of the item under inspection: Pierce (1986) describes the use of automatic speech recognition in fabric inspection at an American manufacturing plant. Inspectors there are now able to save time and to continue scanning and handling the fabric whilst recording any observed faults via the speech recogniser. In addition, because the fault records are being made directly into the computer, paperwork is reduced considerably, and summary statistics for all the observed faults are quickly and easily available. A 25% increase in productivity is claimed as a result of the new technology, and safer working practices have been said to result from the inspector being able to keep her or his eyes on the work.

3.2.2. Applications to the Disabled

The success of the above applications illustrates that when a person's hands and/or eyes are busy, speech provides a useful medium for input to and output from a computer. The same medium is also beneficial in the analogous situation where a person may be paralysed or blind. Damper (1984) has demonstrated the feasibility of using voice input for environmental control: adjusting the lights, heating and electrical appliances in a room simply by issuing spoken commands. For a severely physically disabled person, this is of course a boon. However, that speech-based environmental control is feasible does not necessarily mean it is accessible. The current 'Speech Technology' magazine advertises an environmental control unit for a typical price of $1200: this would tend to put such a unit in the category of 'expensive luxuries' for the majority of disabled persons.

Perhaps one of the greater deprivations suffered by blind persons is not being able to read conventional text. Speech technology has been shown to have benefits in this area as well. The Kurzweil reading machines have been in production for seven years or so, and by optical character recognition are able to effectively read aloud in synthetic speech from a page of normal text. That the synthetic voice attached to these machines is rather strange and robotic does not present too many problems, as the blind person is able to adjust to the voice, and to come to find it entirely comprehensible. Another useful system which can help to keep blind persons in touch is described by Rubenstein (1984). This system, in use in Sweden, allows newspaper text to be transmitted overnight by radio and stored on the blind person's computer for re-synthesis in the morning.

For those with a vocal handicap, speech has the advantages over more conventional visual, often printed, forms of output, that the recipient of the intended message does not have to be in a fixed position in order to receive it. There are a number of speech prostheses available, all of which allow the non-vocal person to type a message that will be subsequently, or simultaneously, 'spoken' by the prosthesis. Devices vary according to the nature of the input they require and the variety of messages they are able to produce. 'Semantic' input requires that the user input some representation of the concept underlying the intended message. A very limited repertoire of messages will result. A much larger number of statements can be produced from a device relying on input from more conventional keyboards, but the speed of communication is consequently reduced. Abbreviated forms of input on a QWERTY keyboard have been experimented with in an attempt to increase the rate of communication; input by machine shorthand such as 'Palantype' may also help to get message composition up to verbatim speed (Arnott & Newell, 1984).

Aids also exist for the deaf and hearing impaired, for whom clearly the most effective aid would be an ASR system that could convert conversational speech into a convenient visual form - text, for example. The ideal speech-to-text system is far from being realised, however. There are currently available a number of 'speech processing' aids which carry out some very limited automatic processing of speech, and display the results either auditorily, tactually or visually (Levitt et al., 1980). Many such aids are used more commonly with pre-lingually deaf children for speech training and correction, rather than for day-to-day communication. One particularly valuable use of speech synthesis is in diagnostic testing of hearing impairment (Wright & Crossley, 1985). The conventional method of carrying this out involves playing a series of tones to the patient at changing levels of amplitude, and having them indicate when the tone is present. Synthetic speech tokens can be used in the place of tones, and have been shown to be consistent in diagnosing the type of hearing impairment, to have more value than tones in predicting the nature of the speech discrimination problems the patient is likely to suffer, and also to facilitate incremental increases in the difficulty of the tests.

3.2.3. Applications in Aviation

There is also particular interest in the use of speech as an I/O medium from designers of aircraft. Modern aircraft cockpits differ markedly from the situations mentioned above, in that the operators, the pilots, are under a very high workload (Berman, 1984). They have many tasks to perform concurrently, often with great time pressure. The large amount of visual information presented to the pilots, coupled with the high demand on their manual resources, means that the pilots' motor and visual channels become overloaded. (The assumption is that, within the range of effort demanded, each channel is effectively supported by an independent and limited source of processing capacity.) With the aim of exploiting the auditory channel, synthesised speech auditory warning signals have been in use for some time in aircraft cockpits, and are particularly suited to attracting the pilot's attention, being easily discriminable both from the array of visual inputs, and from the jumble of speech usually heard over an aircraft's radio (Simpson, 1982).

Aside from speech output, the use of automatic speech recognition in the cockpit is particularly desirable to reduce the competition for resources which exists as a result of the pilot trying to use keyboards and control panels to communicate with the aircraft subsystems, whilst attempting to maintain external vision. The primary goal of using ASR in this situation then, is to reduce workload. To this end, speech commands can be used to replace sequences of keystrokes, serving an equivalent purpose to that of dedicated function keys on a keyboard, whilst allowing pilots to direct their vision elsewhere

(Coler, 1984). There are a number of problems with this, however. One of these is that, with an imperfect speech recogniser, the pilot needs to be given feedback on which words have been recognised, and this can sometimes be distracting. Another problem is that, when a large number of words can potentially be recognised by the system, the pilot has the task of remembering them all. Thus, if the pilot is to remember all the permissible words, his mental load may actually be increased by the introduction of ASR (Taylor, 1986).

The above examples, drawn from a diversity of applications, serve to illustrate that speech I/O is actually being exploited, and in a fairly wide range of applications. They do little, however, to dispel the belief that the technology, even though it is supposedly based on the most natural and convenient means of communication available to us, is not achieving its full potential as a medium for human-computer interaction. Why are our offices not inundated with speech-based dictation machines? Why are telephones dial- or keypad-operated and not voice-operated? And where is the talking, listening computer? It may be that the technology is simply not good enough to fulfil these functions. To test this contention requires an examination of typical performance figures for speech recognisers and speech synthesisers, both in terms of the nature, and of the level of performance.

3.3. TYPICAL PERFORMANCE LEVELS AND CAPABILITIES

3.3.1. Automatic Speech Recognisers

Virtually all commercially available automatic speech recognisers are based on the principle of template-matching. Speech samples are provided by a particular speaker, and are stored digitally by the recogniser. Usually 3-10 samples of each word are required. These samples then provide the reference templates against which all incoming utterances will be matched. An utterance will be recognised as being a particular word, W, in the event that the template for W provides both the closest match to the utterance, and provides a sufficiently close match. The requisite closeness of the match, the 'reject threshold criterion', can be pre-set by the user to suit the characteristics of the task. For most systems, the user has to speak in isolated words, that is with a brief pause between words to identify word boundaries. More systems are now incorporating connected word recognition, however, wherein the inter-word pauses are not necessary, but the speaker must avoid running adjacent words into one another. A few systems also cater for continuous-speech recognition, which allows the user to speak in an almost natural voice. There has also been limited success with speaker-independent systems, which do not require template training by every intended user, and are thus suited to applications in, say, the telephone service. See

Moore (1984) for an overview. [1]

Performance figures for speech recognisers are usually given in terms of the percentage of utterances which are correctly recognised. An utterance which is not recognised can either be 'rejected', whereby it fails to match sufficiently well with any of the templates; or be subject to a 'substitution error', whereby the utterance is matched to the wrong template, and is consequently misrecognised. Average recognition rates are usually quoted by manufacturers as being in the region of 95-99%, and there is generally little variation in this figure amongst devices. The number of words that can be handled by commercially available speech recognisers can be anything up to 1000, but is typically between 50 and 150 at any one time. The overall capacity of a recogniser can be much greater than this, however: only some of the templates need be included in the search for the best match to an incoming utterance. Often, the templates of the words that are extremely unlikely to occur at a given point in the transaction can be excluded from the search at that point.

3.3.2. Speech Synthesisers

There are two main types of speech synthesiser, those based on synthesis-by-analysis, and those based on synthesis-by-rule. The output from these systems differs in terms of two main characteristics: its intelligibility, or how easily it can be understood; and the range of words and phrases that can be produced.

Synthesis-by-analysis is the process that applies to most low-cost, on-chip synthesisers. The parameters that are required to generate a particular speech segment from the synthesiser are derived from an analysis of features of a sample of that speech sound. The parameters are digitally encoded, and can be stored for subsequent re-synthesis. These parameters represent the pitch, energy and type of speech sound, and can be stored in Read Only Memory (ROM) at a typical rate of 2000 bits per second of speech. It is the on-chip, synthesis-by-analysis devices that are used in most low-cost, commercial applications. For example, in the talking BL Maestro car (Redpath, 1984), in home computers and in toys. The quality of speech produced by this type of synthesiser is variously described as 'robotic' or 'noticeably synthetic'. Also, the available vocabulary is very limited: a 64Kbit ROM can only store about 120 seconds of speech. Assuming an average 0.6 s per word, this amounts to a total vocabulary of only 200 words: a rather inarticulate system.

Synthesis-by-rule is the process by which the above synthesisers can

---

[1] A new generation of speech recognisers is currently emerging which is based on phoneme recognition. These are mentioned later.

be driven in real time, and with an unlimited vocabulary. This is enabled by text-to-speech software, which effectively provides the rules by which any ASCII input can be translated into synthesiser parameters, and subsequently be 'spoken'. Thus a custom vocabulary of encoded speech is not necessary. The quality of the speech produced in this way is generally less than that of the above, and although their vocabulary may be unlimited, text-to-speech systems are prone to mispronounce uncommon words and proper nouns. (To guard against this, the software can be made to incorporate a 'dictionary' of exceptions to normal pronunciation.) In addition, the intonation of the speech may not be as natural as that in synthesis-by-analysis, as this has also to be calculated from a limited size rule base.

3.4. TYPES OF PERFORMANCE MEASURE

There is some doubt as to the validity of the measures mentioned above which characterise the performance of speech I/O devices. Firstly, what is meant by the intelligibility of synthetic speech ? Subjective judgements of intelligibility are bound to vary from person to person, and will hinge both on the familiarity of the speech sample and the character ascribed to it by listeners. Also, the quality of speech judged to be acceptable will vary according to its application: what may be judged an acceptable voice for a child's toy may not be considered suitable for making announcements over the telephone. Objectively, intelligibility is extremely hard to quantify: what are the units of intelligibility, and how can comparisons be made amongst different devices, such that one could state that a particular synthesiser was 'twice as intelligible' or 'half as easy to understand' as another?

There is similarly some doubt as to the validity of the idea of using a single figure to describe speech recogniser performance. It does not indicate the probability of extra-vocabulary words being rejected by the system, in the event, for example, that the user is not aware of the content of the permitted vocabulary. [2] But neither does it allow reliable comparisons to be made amongst a range of devices. If a figure of, say, 95% is quoted as the recognition accuracy of a device, with how much confidence can that device be said to be as good as another with a similar percentage recognition rate? To arrive at a percentage figure such as this, one has to operate the speech recogniser with a reasonable number of speakers, and to record the proportion of occasions on which correct word recognition takes place. What are

---

[2] One way of producing impressive recognition figures for a speech recogniser is to use a high value for the recognition threshold. Thus, very few utterances will actually be matched to any template, i.e. there will be many rejections, but virtually all the matches will be correct ones, and the rate of matches can be quoted as 99% or so.

not included with the recogniser performance figures are details of the
population of speakers with whom the given figures were obtained:
their dialect, sex, age, etc, the conditions under which the figures
were arrived at, in terms of ambient noise levels, the type of microphone used, whether it was fitted with an on/off switch and in what
position it was used, length of the test session, etc, and more importantly, the vocabulary of words which formed the material for the
test. All of these factors have been found to significantly affect
recogniser performance (Lea, 1980), and cannot be relied upon to be
the same in a task situation involving the use of ASR, as in the
laboratory-controlled situation in which the recognition figures were
calculated.

A problem that arises from the lack of valid performance measures is
that potential users of speech technology, who have never encountered a working device directly, do not have a realistic idea of how
efficiently it can be expected to work. This is one factor contributing
to the myth of speech technology, and may even be a factor in creating a type of positive feedback loop whereby low confidence in a
speech-based system may actually produce, as well as be produced
by, low levels of system performance. Before examining why this
should be, it serves to consider some evidence regarding the degree to
which currently achievable performance levels of both speech recognition and speech synthesis accord with people's expectations.

3.5. WHAT IS EXPECTED OF THE TECHNOLOGY ?

3.5.1. Automatic Speech Recognition

Two important factors in using automatic speech recognition are
the type of word input, whether it is in isolated words or in continuous speech, and the number of different words that can be handled
by the system. The influence of these factors can be shown by reference to an hypothesised speech-driven dictating system: a fairly ambitious project, although a good example as it does not contain the spe-
cialisms of the examples of applications given above.

Firstly, one consideration which will have a bearing on the users'
opinion of the system is the manner, isolated or continuous, in which
it will accept the spoken items. The production rate of the system
will be considerably affected by this feature: consider that an experienced typist can type at around 55-75 words per minute, compared
with the 100 words per minute that could be achieved by the error-
free listening typewriter working with continuous speech input. If the
system could only recognise speech when it was spoken in isolated
words, this would slow the rate down to around 20-40 words per
minute (based on typical response latencies for ASR systems).

Secondly, the number of words allowed by the system would significantly affect its usefulness. Around 75% of most non-specialist text is composed from the 1000 most frequent words in the English language; about 95% of text is composed from the most frequent 5000 words (the remaining 5% in general being particular to the subject of the text). Bearing in mind that a typist would be able to type 100% of the words dictated to him or her, then anything less than the 5000 word capacity for the listening typewriter, with a spelling option for the specialist words, would probably be unsatisfactory.

Thus, it may be predicted from arguments such as these what sort of a speech recognition system people might expect for word processing. In a test of this type of prediction, Gould et al. (1982) constructed a simulation of a listening typewriter. They varied the number of words that the system could recognise, and also the nature of word input (either in isolated words, or in continuous speech), and required subjects to dictate to the system as they would normally dictate letters. The subjects expressed dissatisfaction with a 1000 word vocabulary, even though this is the largest that is currently realisable in a listening typewriter, and strongly preferred to have an unlimited vocabulary. They also considered that the vocabulary size was a more important factor than the nature of word input, i.e that continuous speech would be preferable, but they could tolerate speaking in isolated words provided all the words would then be recognised. This simulation illustrates quite clearly that people's expectations for a listening typewriter are considerably beyond what is actually realisable at the moment. However, as noted earlier, this particular application is not ideally suited to the use of ASR, and so a different picture may have emerged had the simulation been of an inspection line, or had disabled persons comprised the sample population.

3.5.2. Speech Synthesis

An analogous example to the above is in using a speech synthesiser for reading out unrestricted, non-specialist text. In such an application, it might be predicted that listeners would require an unlimited vocabulary, and an easily comprehensible and friendly voice. Such predictions have been tested, to an extent, by Edman and Metz (1983). They assessed a group of office worker's reactions to samples of natural speech and to samples of a digitised version of the same speech. (The digitised version was comparable to very high quality synthetic speech, as the intonation contours, pitch and rate of the natural speech would have been largely preserved.) They found that even with this high degree of speech quality, subjects rejected the synthesised voice as being too 'choppy' and 'machine-like'. Other features of synthetic voices were highlighted by Michaelis and Wiggins (1982), who found that unfamiliar synthesisers were rated by listeners as being 'evil' and 'sinister'.

These studies show the dimensions along which listeners who do have an adverse reaction to synthetic speech tend to describe their dislike for it. Clearly, the actual value of the ratings one could expect to obtain would be heavily dependent on the actual synthesiser under test, and so no firm conclusions can be drawn about reactions to synthetic speech in general. There are many facets to a particular voice: its rate, pitch and intonation pattern being a few which can be objectively stated, and its ascribed age, gender and character being somewhat more difficult to measure objectively, but no less real to listeners. It would appear from various studies, not least those carried out by myself, that aspects of the character listeners ascribe to a voice are equally salient in their judgements of its quality as are the voice's more objective features. Moreover, listeners tend to overestimate the extent to which such aspects can be adjusted to suit particular tastes.

3.6. DISPELLING THE MYTH

It is clear that many people have expectations of speech technology, especially of automatic speech recognition, that go far beyond what is currently attainable. This must be a significant factor in the perpetuation of the myth of speech technology. One result of this is the creation of a paradoxical situation whereby people who hold realistically high expectations when they come to use speech I/O may actually obtain worse performance from it than other users holding no such expectations.

The reason for this paradox is that users who do not have an accurate model of how well the speech interface can perform tend to initially overestimate its performance, and this leads to a lack of confidence or satisfaction in the system upon realising its true limitations. In the case of ASR, lowering of users' confidence and/or motivation below a certain threshold has been found to actually affect their diction to the extent of having an adverse effect on recognition performance (Martin & Welch, 1980). In the case of synthetic speech output, it would seem that (all too common) dissatisfaction with the quality of a synthetic voice may result in a lowering of motivation to comprehend it. It has been established that more cognitive effort (more mental processing) is required to understand synthetic speech (Waterworth & Thomas, 1985; Talbot, this volume), and the additional effort is unlikely to be applied by an unmotivated listener.

This paradox leads to a situation where the outcome of expecting too much from speech I/O is that one will actually get less out of it. However, the extent to which this is true will depend on the particular application and the potential benefits of introducing speech I/O into it. In the example of the hypothesised listening typewriter, little would be gained by its introduction, as word processors are available for a fraction of the cost which do the job equally well, if not better. Thus, the benefits of introducing ASR are few, the expectations of the potential users, as identified in the Gould et al. (1982) study, far exceed what is achievable, and hence the above paradox would be most in evidence. On the other hand, taking the example of a speech-driven aid for a severely physically disabled person, even being able to operate by speech an environmental control system to adjust the temperature and lights, etc. would make significant improvements to their quality of life. This would only require that the unit recognise about 10-15 isolated words: a requirement well within even the most pessimistic expectations. So in this case, the benefits due to ASR are great, the expectations are low relative to what is actually possible, and so the paradox will not be so much in evidence.

A significant step towards improving the accuracy of the user population's model of the capabilities of speech I/O would appear to be the development of an improved set of performance measures. Not only would this reduce the effects of lowered confidence described above, but it might also serve to assist users in their choice of application for the technology, avoiding inappropriate or overambitious projects. This in turn might well increase the general efficiency of speech-based human-computer systems. The following section suggests the foundations for some such measures.

3.7. TOWARDS IMPROVED PERFORMANCE MEASURES

Two broad types of performance measures relevant to speech I/O can be identified:

(1)   Those which allow comparisons amongst devices in terms of how well they carry out their immediate function, i.e. accurately recognising human speech and accurately synthesising human-like speech.

(2)   Those which provide a more pragmatic indication of whether a particular application or interface will benefit from the introduction of speech I/O.

Within each of these types, which measures are appropriate will depend on whether it is speech input or output under consideration.

3.7.1. Speech Input Performance

As mentioned earlier, 'percentage recognition rate', P, is the most frequently quoted index of speech recognition performance. However, consider just some of the factors that will affect the tests which are used to arrive at this figure:

(1)   The nature of the words in the vocabulary: acoustically similar words (such as bean and beam) will cause more substitution errors, and a consequent lowering of P (Green & Clark, 1981).

(2)   The speakers used in the tests: there is considerable between-speaker variation in recognition figures, especially due to the sex of the speaker. Females are typically less well recognised than males (DeGeorge, 1981; Waterworth, 1984).

(3)   The procedure for creating the voice templates: the number of times each word is uttered, the order in which the words are repeated and the pace of the temkplate creation procedure will all affect P (Conolly, 1977; Martin & Welch, 1980).

Clearly, to standardise tests which are designed to evaluate P, the above factors must be held constant. Russell et al., (1983) have constructed a speech database with the aim of achieving that constancy. They used fifteen speakers, both male and female, whose voices represented a range of regional accents. Each subject spoke, under controlled conditions and using high quality recording equipment, a standard set of 288 words in 16 different random orderings. The recording sessions also included speech affected by controlled variations in speech level and rate, amongst other factors.

What Russell et al. produced constitutes a comprehensive, representative and invariant collection of samples of the human voice, which can be used to train and operate a variety of speech recognisers in a range of conditions of noise and bandwidth limitations, etc. The use of this database would appear to overcome the problem of standardisation of testing procedures for speech recognisers. However, the goal of using the database is still to arrive at a figure for the percentage recognition rate of a device. Quoting this figure for a particular ASR device does not provide an indication as to its efficiency relative to alternative methods of data input, nor does it indicate what the performance levels might be in less controlled and constrained testing conditions, for example in the presence of background noise or of stressful task demands.

What would be preferable to this measure would be something more pragmatic, that could be evaluated relative to some system equivalent to an ASR device. Peckham (1984) proposes the metric, 'Transaction Time' as a suitable measure, it being the time a user must spend on a speech-based transaction before he or she is satisfied with the result. The value of this measure is that it could possibly be used to make comparisons with alternative, tactile, input methods. It is, however, rather a large unit to use for finer comparisons, and is too prone to variations between judges in what constitutes 'satisfaction' with a result. It would perhaps be more profitable if the transaction task were broken down into its sub-components, and comparisons made on the time to complete each of these. Another comparative measure is proposed by Moore (1977). This is a standard for evaluating speech recognisers relative to human word recognition performance: it is based on the principle that human ability for word recognition will decrease as a function of the amount of ambient noise in the listening environment. By modelling the extent of that decrease in proportion to the observed signal-to-noise ratio, Moore proposes that automatic speech recogniser performance can be described in terms of the Human Equivalent Noise Ratio, or HENR. A high value of HENR would indicate poor recogniser performance.

HENR would appear to be a fairly valid index of speech recogniser performance, at least for the purpose of comparing different models or versions of recognisers. Such comparisons will be most useful to designers and manufacturers of the technology, who need to test systems to evaluate the effects of design changes, etc. HENR would also be useful for testing the effects on recognition rates of altering the microphone used, of providing feedback to the talker on recognition performance, or on altering the level of background noise, etc.

However, for someone thinking of replacing or updating some existing human-computer interface with speech I/O, it does little to help. It would not, for example, indicate what overall benefits might be gained from the incorporation of speech input into a particular task. A more satisfactory solution to this would be to perform a combination of cost analysis and task analysis on the system in question, both before and after the introduction of speech input. The former would take into account the cost of recognition errors made by the ASR device; the cost of training personnel on the new system; and the cost of the hardware and software necessary to undergo a conversion to speech. The latter would revolve around the effect of the new system on worker satisfaction (both of the worker directly concerned and of her or his colleagues); on the reduction (or otherwise) in the physical and mental loading of operators; and ultimately on the speed with which the task in question could be performed. Available reports on such task analyses typically show that, for data entry tasks, the most efficient system is one which uses a combination of voice and manual data entry, although of course this will depend on the nature of the task (Martin & Welch, 1980); while for situations in which there is a relatively small vocabulary of entries and a concurrent manual task, data entry by way of ASR alone is the most efficient method (Visick et al., 1984).

3.7.2. Speech Output Performance

Accepted and universal measures of the quality of synthetic speech are few. This is illustrated by the fact that manufacturers of speech synthesisers generally omit to include any indication of quality or intelligibility in advertisements for their products. (See any issue of

'Speech Technology' magazine.) That is not to say that intelligibility metrics do not exist.

The extent to which synthetic speech can be said to be intelligible may be indicated by two measures. Firstly, intelligibility will depend on the extent to which individual speech sounds which are close in the perceptual space can be discriminated by listeners when 'spoken' by the synthesiser. Secondly, intelligibility will depend on the extent to which samples of the synthesiser's fluent speech can be comprehended by listeners, or if total comprehension is possible, how much effort this process requires. The ability to discriminate a synthesiser's speech sounds can be assessed by means of the Diagnostic Rhyme Test (DRT) (Voiers, 1983). The tests of fluent speech comprehension can be carried out by requiring listeners to attend to selected passages of speech, and requiring them to carry out subsequent or concurrent tasks relating to the passages.

The distinction between these two types of tests is in terms of the amount of a priori uncertainty present at the time of judging the identity of a speech sound. In the DRT, any extraneous information as to that identity is minimised. The procedure of the DRT is that the listener is presented visually with two words, which differ only with respect to their initial consonant: 'meat' and 'beat', for example, or 'key' and 'tea'. One of these words (the choice is random) is then spoken by the synthesiser, and the listener has to make a decision as to which word has just been heard. Thus no information is available to the listener other than that carried in the synthetic speech signal. In contrast, performance on the second type of task is facilitated by contextual information. This is the information which allows a listener, on the basis of hearing part of a sentence, to guess as to the remainder of that sentence. The procedure in this test is that subjects hear a series of phrases spoken by the synthesiser. After each phrase, they have to repeat back what they think they have heard.

The scores which result from the DRT, in units of 'percentage correct discriminations' indicate which speech sounds are well enunciated by the synthesiser, and which may be easily confused. (Hence the *Diagnostic* Rhyme Test.) These results will be useful from two perspectives: firstly, to indicate where the synthesis algorithm is weak, and so to aid its development; and secondly to assist in the design of the dialogue or messages to be spoken by the synthesiser: the DRT will indicate which phrases might be ambiguous and hence should be excluded.

From the listen-and-repeat test, the scores, in terms of 'percentage of words correctly repeated', indicate the intelligibility of fluent samples of the synthetic speech. These scores thus take some account of the intonation patterns, the pitch and the rate of the synthetic voice.

However, more fine-grained evaluation of particular features of a synthetic voice is sometimes required, particularly during the process of synthesiser development, and the above measures are not necessarily sensitive enough for such tests. For this purpose, it is necessary to take a closer look at the way the human listener carries out word recognition, and how this process is affected, at a word level, by the synthesis algorithm. Account can also be taken, in a well-designed evaluation, of such aspects of the speech signal as its bandwidth and the level of context provided. Ultimately, the amount of effort that a listener has to bring to bear on the word recognition process in order to carry out a set task will provide the best measure of the intelligibility of a speech sample. That human speech understanding requires so little effort on the part of the listener means that subjective judgements of this are bound to be inaccurate and spurious, and so objective measurements are preferred. These can be obtained through standard and well established paradigms such as reaction time measurement (e.g. Foss, 1969), or the use of a secondary task (e.g. Rabbitt, 1968).

As before, certain applications will require that an evaluation is made, not only of the finer aspects of the synthetic speech signal itself, but of the effect of incorporating it into a particular task or interface. How does it alter transaction times and error rates on the task ? How does it affect the well-being of the operator and those who work with him or her ?

3.8. THE FUTURE OF SPEECH TECHNOLOGY

A number of the capabilities and attributes that are commonly ascribed to speech technology have been shown to be fallacious, or in general to be overestimates. It may be the case, however, that many of the expectations that are held about the technology could come to be realised some time in the future. It is appropriate, then, to conclude by considering the present direction of developments, and to speculate on how speech I/O and its applications are likely to evolve between now and the end of century.

3.8.1. Developments in Speech Recognition

Possibly the most significant single development in the technology of automatic speech recognition is that of phonetic speech recognition. The automatic speech recognisers discussed above, which have been commercially available for ten years or so, are almost without exception based on the storage and matching of spectrographic representations of whole words. The problems with this approach are covered in detail elsewhere in this volume, but are essentially:

(1)   The vocabulary of words which are to be recognised must be chosen such that they are acoustically dissimilar. This limits the size of the vocabulary that can be used.

(2)   For each word that is to be recognised, the talker must provide several spoken samples, in order that the recognition system can create the spectrographic representation (template) for it.

(3)   During recognition, the words have to be spoken very consistently in terms of pitch, duration and volume.

(4)   The words have to be spoken in isolation, such that adjacent words do not run into one another.

These problems arise because of the largeness of the units which are being stored and matched. (Consider how the problems would be exacerbated if the units of recognition were whole sentences.) They could be alleviated, in theory, if units smaller than a word were to form the basis of the recognition process.

The phonetic recognition approach tackles the above shortcomings by storing and matching phonemes, thereby inferring the recognised words, rather than directly matching the words themselves. Thus, the 'training' of a phonetic recogniser consists of the speaker providing samples of the 40 minimal speech units. This means the training phase will be shorter than for a comparable word-recogniser. Words are subsequently recognised as being various combinations of these units. This approach means that the constraint on the dissimilarity of the words in the vocabulary is lessened. In theory, words will not be classified as the same provided they differ in terms of at least one phoneme. The other shortcomings of word-level recognisers are also variously alleviated by the phonetic recognition approach. Much of the variability in pitch and duration encountered during the recognition process can be allowed for during training by having the talker provide a number of different samples of each phoneme. Also, if algorithms are used to extract samples of the phonemes from a number of phonetic environments, variations brought about by the nature of the surrounding sounds will be accounted for. More significantly, by drawing on stored knowledge of phonology and syntax, an efficient phonetic recogniser will be able to handle strings of words spoken without exaggerated pauses at their boundaries. These boundaries will be inferred from knowledge of permissible combinations of phonemes, rather than being detected by the identification of a particular-length silent period.

On a theoretical note, it is significant that the more effective approach exemplified by phonetic recognition is more alike the *human* word recognition process than is whole-word recognition (Barry, 1984). The success demonstrated by whole-word speech recognition systems of the last decade, which have essentially used rudimentary techniques of pattern recognition, has been rather limited. The new generation of speech recognisers, however, has abandoned this engineering-type approach in favour of emulation of the human word recognition process, and has also favoured the use of encoded knowledge about the characteristics of human speech to facilitate recognition. Assuming that the predictions about the high performance of phonetic recognisers are borne out, the message of this shift in emphasis has to be that in order to build into a machine the capacity for automatically carrying out a human function, the algorithms and the knowledge base used by humans in performing that function need to be closely imitated, not substituted for. The further development of even more efficient speech recognisers could perhaps benefit from making use of such a principle.

There are not yet any commercially available phonetic recognisers. One manufacturer, Speech Systems Incorporated of California, is about to produce a large vocabulary 'talkwriter', based on phonetic recognition and accepting continuous speech input. Other manufacturers have systems at the development stage. The advent of these systems is likely to herald a considerable advance in the capabilities of automatic speech recognition. This is likely to bring about a large increase in the number and extent of applications of speech recognition. Aside from there being an increase in the extent to which speech recognition is used in existing applications, it is feasible that speech recognition will come to be incorporated into some programming tasks, into computer-aided design and manufacture, into telephone access of databases, and into many other applications satisfying the criteria mentioned earlier (hands and eyes occupied, etc.). In addition, the manner of operation of the speech recognisers will evolve. Further into the future, systems may come about which will incorporate an encoded model of spoken language which is generalised across talkers and even across languages. Ultimately, the general-language, natural speech, listening typewriter will be produced. This will not require any training of the templates, except perhaps for defining the gross characteristics of the particular talker's voice; it will transcribe, in real time, a spoken version of any language to a written version of any other language without the need for the speaker to make any more effort than if he or she were talking to a fellow human.

3.8.2. Developments in Speech Synthesis

Fairly high quality, unlimited vocabulary synthetic speech can currently be produced by devices on the basis of a relatively unrestricted version of text input. This is evidence that text-to-speech algorithms are at an advanced stage of development, and, as far as the fluent production of American English goes, are perfectly adequate. In addition to this, chips enabling smaller vocabularies of stored speech (using synthesis-by-analysis) are readily available, and are suitable for incorporation into many practical settings, some of which were mentioned earlier.

Thus, relative to the technology of automatic speech recognition, speech synthesis is at an advanced stage of development. However, it is clear that synthetic speech remains less comprehensible than natural speech, and so there are still areas where significant amounts of work need to be done. For example, an important aspect of the quality of synthetic speech is its intonation, although this factor has been largely glossed over in the development of many synthetic voices. Work is currently in progress (Silverman, 1985) which is seeking to improve the intonation of synthetic speech and thus to make it more acceptable to listeners. The research tackles the problem of intonation at several levels: at the level of the segment, such that pitch cues as to phoneme identity are correctly reproduced; at the level of the utterance, such that the the intonation contour within a sentence is made more natural; and also at the discourse level, enabling the synthetic speech to convey information about turn-taking and the location in a sentence of salient information. (It is conceivable that, if speech recognition were to reach a more advanced state of development, it too could use an analysis of patterns of the pitch and timing of speech in order to aid recognition.)

Besides making improvements to the intrinsic intelligibility and naturalness of synthetic speech, future developments will centre on increasing the range of languages which can be synthesised. There is, as yet, no synthesiser of British English which is as high in quality as the synthesisers of American English. This situation is likely to change before the end of the century. Also, synthesisers can only produce one language each. A significant advancement would be a synthesiser which could accept text in any language and convert it to a spoken form of that language with all the idiosyncratic features of that language correctly specified. Ultimately, a speech synthesiser would be able to produce speech in a number of languages given a standard set of input symbols not specific to any language. This would also enable it to translate amongst languages. However, this would require that some set of universals be identified which are common to all languages. Effectively, this would mean the development of some system of specifying one's meaning and intentions to the synthesiser, and it then selecting the right spoken message to convey them. Such an achievement will not be made in the foreseeable future, if at all.

Regarding developments this century in the *applications* of synthetic speech, it is likely that reductions in cost and/or increases in the available speech quality will lead to a greater proliferation of speech output in many areas. As text-to-speech algorithms become more advanced and more widely available, unlimited-vocabulary speech may be incorporated into word-processing tasks, for reading back drafts of documents or abstracts of papers; into information services where the information is being constantly updated, such as weather forecasts, traffic news and stock exchange information; and into such consumer items as games and domestic appliances. For applications which do not require, or benefit from, unlimited vocabulary speech, the currently decreasing price and increasing density of memory will enable a much wider usage of stored speech. Simgle- or multi-chip systems will allow speech to be added cheaply to, for example, user manuals for consumer products, vending machines (this has already begun), cash dispensers, and so on.

3.9. CONCLUSIONS

The myth of speech technology can at least be partly shattered by a consideration of how the technology is currently serving a useful purpose in a variety of applications. Apart from a lack of awareness of these cases, another reason for the existence of the myth is the lack of reliable and accepted performance measures for speech I/O. Adequate performance measures are desirable because they can contribute to an accurate model of the technology's full capabilities, and as such might actually help users to get the most out of it. Chapter 4 outlines the background to a new metric of speech output performance, based on listeners' reaction times. Chapter 5 discusses ways in which the performance of simple speech recognition devices can be enhanced, by improved 'training' regimes for the capture of speakers' voice samples.

For ASR devices, existing measures of performance have little practical value, and in the case of speech synthesis, although some measures do exist, they tend not to be applied by manufacturers. Assessment of the finer points of a particular synthetic voice requires an analysis of listeners' perception of it in terms of the cognitive effort it requires, or the speed at which word recognition can be carried out on it. However, the usefulness of using either a speech recogniser or a speech synthesiser can best be assessed through a combination of task analysis and cost analysis.

The future of speech technology was discussed, and it is clear that advancements in all areas are likely to be seen before the end of the century. The quality of synthetic speech and the accuracy of speech recognisers wil improve, and the products will become more widely available. Considering the technology as of the present day, from the examples quoted and the measures and performance levels discussed in this chapter, the conclusion should be that speech technology is not a panacea, and has not yet evolved to suit such tasks as text composition or automatic, real-time speech transcription. However, in certain applications, it already has great advantages over the tactile and visual modalities, and for disabled people, where these modalities are impaired or completely lacking, is indispensable.

4

Reaction Time as a Metric for the Intelligibility of Synthetic Speech

M. Talbot

4.1. INTRODUCTION

In applications where the merits of various types of speech need to be compared and evaluated, for example in the development of speech synthesisers, it is important to have consistent and appropriate metrics of intelligibility or quality (see Talbot, 1985). However, the concept of speech intelligibility is elusive, and its measurement particularly difficult. It is proposed that, with the goal of defining a metric of speech intelligibility and developing suitable testing techniques for its measurement, the following requirements should ideally be met:

(1) Validity: it must be demonstrable that the metric actually measures speech intelligibility, and not some other feature incidental to the conditions under which the speech is tested; subjective preferences for the supposed 'character' of the speech, for example. A metric which claims to be valid must, therefore, include a particular definition of intelligibility.

(2) Reliability: to have any predictive value, the value obtained for the intelligibility metric when testing a particular speech sample must be replicated upon repeated testing. This will generally apply to re-testing with different groups of listeners. A metric which is valid, according to the above definition, is likely also to be reliable.

(3)   Parsimony: speech intelligibility is inevitably defined relative to human speech processing performance. The model of performance upon which an intelligibility metric is based must be robust. As a rule, this means that it should rely on as few assumptions as possible regarding the psychological mechanisms underlying the processing of the speech by the listener.

Arriving at a suitable metric for the intelligibility of speech will inevitably raise questions regarding why certain types of speech are less intelligible than others. If one's goal is to make synthetic speech more intelligible to a human listener, one needs to know not only about the characteristics of the sounds produced by the synthesiser, but also about how these interact with the psychological mechanisms a listener brings to bear on the speech understanding process. More formally, the reasons for differences in intelligibility should be explained in terms of three levels of description:

(1)   The sounds carried by the speech, the *phonological* code;

(2)   The contribution made to the process by the listener's internal representation of meanings conveyed by the speech, the *semantic* code;

(3)   The listener's knowledge of the means of relating the two, that is, of the language's *syntactic system*.

The present study has two goals. Firstly, by carrying out a reaction time experiment using various types of speech, it is hoped to develop an index of intelligibility to meet the above criteria. Secondly, it is intended to speculate on the ways in which sound and knowledge interact when a listener attempts to recognise words carried in an impoverished speech signal. Previous attempts to investigate this latter question are first discussed.

4.1.1. Previous Work

Various paradigms have been used in the past to investigate speech processing from two different perspectives: firstly, to determine the nature of the psychological mechanisms involved in processing normal speech; and secondly, in attempting to discover the reasons why degraded or synthesised speech requires more cognitive effort than its natural counterpart. Studies have typically concentrated on listeners' ability to carry out secondary tasks whilst processing that speech, or on listeners' memory for that speech. A limited number of studies have used reaction time as an index of intelligibility. Rabbitt (1966) investigated the increase in the amount of cognitive effort required to process speech when it was played over a noisy channel. This was achieved by employing a secondary task paradigm. Listeners were required to shadow a spoken list of words (to repeat the list items back verbatim in real time) whilst retaining in memory items from an earlier list. The listeners were required to indicate when they heard a word that had occurred on the earlier list. Thus, listeners were performing the primary task of listening to, and shadowing, the current word list; while their secondary task was remembering the earlier list. It was found that the efficiency of identification of the remembered words, and the confidence with which listeners made judgements, were both lessened when the to-be-remembered list was presented through noise. Assuming that the listeners were bringing to bear on the two tasks a limited amount of cognitive effort (e.g. Broadbent, 1958; Deutsch & Deutsch, 1963), and that the two tasks were competing for that effort, then an explanation for Rabbitt's result would be that the increased effort of decoding the noisy words reduced the spare capacity for the operation of remembering them. Rabbitt (1968) then tried a similar paradigm, but using prose instead of isolated words. This time the latter half of the passage was played through noise, and it was found that, under this condition, the early half was less well recalled than when the whole passage was played in clear conditions. This indicated that the increased difficulty of comprehending the later, noisy speech competed for the available processing capacity, and so interfered with the process of maintaining the earlier information in memory.

The effects observed by Rabbitt using secondary task methodology are analogous to those found in studies of synthetic speech which have used memory performance as the dependent variable. These were discussed in Chapter 2 and will only be briefly described here. Luce et al., (1983) found that when subjects were required to recall in the correct order items from natural and synthetic words lists, that the differences between the efficiency of recall for the two speech types was greater for the primacy portion of the serial position curve than for the recency portion. This was taken to be indicative of the synthetic speech placing an increased demand on encoding and/or rehearsal processes in short-term memory. (Whereas Rabbitt demonstrated that earlier parts of the prose are less well remembered if followed by noise-degraded prose, the result here is that early *synthetic* items are forgotten if followed by further to-be-remembered synthetic items.) The precise stage of the sequence of encoding, rehearsal and recall which produced the deficit was not identified by Luce et al., nor by Rabbitt. However, Waterworth and Thomas (1985), in a replication of Luce et al.'s study, controlled for the effect of erroneous encoding by requiring listeners to repeat aloud the items as they were presented. This allowed them to posit that the difficulty exists at the encoding stage of the process, and that once the synthetic items are correctly encoded, they are no less well remembered than natural speech items. However, Waterworth and Thomas (1985) did find that it was the *recency* portion of the serial position curve that was differentially depressed for the synthetic speech, compared with Luce et al.'s result of the differential primacy effect. This indicated that there is apparently some flexibility in how listeners allocate resources between the encoding and rehearsal of stimuli in short-term memory.

The type of rehearsal strategy adopted by subjects in retaining the speech items in memory might have affected the results in Waterworth and Thomas' (1985) study. To investigate this, two further experiments, described in Waterworth and Holmes (1986), were carried out (see also Chapter 2). The first of these involved a similar task to the above, but using a running memory task instead of lists of known length. This procedure deliberately omitted to inform listeners at what point presentation of the synthetic speech stimuli would stop and their recall would begin. The results from this experiment again indicated that the memory deficit for the synthetic speech items was due to encoding difficulties and not to difficulties, irrespective of the listeners' strategy, to maintain the items in memory. A second experiment, in a similar vein, examined the effect on memory performance of varying the delay between the end of the list of items and the time of recall. The stimuli here were complete sentences which were either meaningful or nonsense. This experiment took account of the different strategies, as identified by Mazuryk and Lockhart (1974), that might be used by listeners when rehearsing the items in memory. Such a distinction considers whether listeners, having heard a list of to-be-remembered items, merely repeat the items to themselves (maintenance rehearsal), or whether they generate associates of the items in order to improve their memory of them (elaborative rehearsal). In this second experiment, sentences, instead of isolated words, were used as stimuli, and listeners were required to memorise and then recall them in one of three conditions: immediately after they had been heard, after a fixed delay which was filled with a task designed to prevent maintenance rehearsal, or after a delay with no fill-in task. It was found that, compared to Waterworth and Thomas's (1985) result, listeners appeared to be allocating greater priority to encoding the stimuli. This is taken to be due to the difference in the stimulus types: whereas Waterworth and Thomas's (1985) stimuli were lists of isolated words, the stimuli in the later experiment were complete sentences, and listeners may have been attempting to encode the entire sentence before executing any rehearsal. The type of rehearsal that subjects were engaging in seems also to have been affected by the recall condition: maintenance rehearsal was adopted by listeners whenever possible (in the immediate recall and unfilled delay conditions), but rehearsal was prevented when the delay before recall was filled with another task.

These memory studies may be summarised by stating that, in general, synthetic speech items are more difficult to encode than natural speech items, but no less difficult to rehearse once encoded; and that less maintenance rehearsal is carried out on encoded synthetic speech items than on natural items, due to the greater allocation of resources to encoding of the former. However, this conclusion does not assist in arriving at an intelligibility metric for synthetic speech. Although synthetic speech may be harder to encode, the extent to which this is the case is not known: is it twice or three times as hard, and what are the units of encoding difficulty anyway ? It would be extremely difficult to try and establish such a figure, as the encoding, rehearsal and recall stages of memory seem to be differentially and unpredictably affected by the type of material and the nature of the memory task used. That the theory of memory performance relies on many assumptions about the nature and degree of various types of processing would also tend, on the principle of parsimony, to lessen its value as an intelligibility measure. Moreover, that memory for speech necessarily relies testing the subject *after* the requisite processing has been carried out on the stimuli suggests that it would not be as sensitive as a measure that tracked cognitive processes *as* they occur. This would imply that the precise measurement of the time course of speech processing would provide much more information to assist the development of an intelligibility metric.

Reaction time has been used in the past to assess speech intelligibility through an examination of certain aspects of word recognition. Pratt (1981), in a study comparing the intelligibility of speech played at different signal to noise ratios, measured the reaction times of listeners carrying out the Modified Rhyme Test. (This test requires that listeners attend to an isolated spoken word, and then choose from five visually presented alternatives which word it was they heard.) Pratt found that when the reaction times of listeners making their choice from the alternatives was analysed along with the correctness of those choices, the discrimination amongst the various speech signals was made more sensitive.

Using reaction time measurement in a different way, Pisoni (1981) required listeners to attend to spoken stimuli and to make a judgement as to whether each stimulus constituted a real word. This lexical decision task was carried out using both natural and synthetic speech items, and it was found that decision times were longer for synthetic items, and for non-words. However, no interaction was observed with speech type and stimulus type, indicating that the difference between words and non-words was similar for both speech types. Assuming that lexical decisions take part in two stages: (1) deriving a phonetic code for the stimulus without any consideration for whether or not it constitutes a word, and then (2) searching a mental lexicon for the stimulus on the basis of that code (Cole & Jakimik, 1980), the implication from this study is that the increase in lexical decision time for synthetic items is due to increased difficulty at the stage of decoding the stimulus prior to lexical look-up, a process which is not affected by lexical status, rather than at the stage of look-up itself, which is. In other words, deriving the phonetic code for a synthetic speech item takes longer than for a natural speech item, but once this has been done, the time taken for lexical look-up is the same for both speech types. Based on word recognition scores, Schwab et al. (1985) found that listeners' ability to comprehend synthetic speech improved with training, both in the short term and over a six-month period, presumably due to an improvement in their ability to carry out this preliminary phonetic analysis.

The above studies show a reliable increase in reaction time for word recognition when the signal is somehow degraded, and provide some evidence that this is brought about by an increase in the effort required to execute a preliminary analysis of the speech stimulus. To establish more accurately the locus of the difficulty in recognising words in a degraded signal, it helps to consider the role of various knowledge sources in the process. In addition to having knowledge about the acoustics of speech, listeners bring to bear on the process of word recognition tacit knowledge of syntax and semantics, which both reduces the time taken to recognise words, and enables them to be predicted before they occur. In a syntactically correct sentence it can be predicted, for example, that a verb often follows the subject of a sentence, or an adverb often follows a verb. From semantic knowledge, a listener is aware of which word combinations constitute meaningful sentences. There is considerable evidence that syntactic and semantic information play a significant role in word recognition and speech perception, although there is some debate over the timing of the knowledge sources. For example, whereas Marslen-Wilson and Tyler (1980) view the process as relying on the interaction of all levels of knowledge at all times, contending that words are recognised *as* they are heard, others (Fodor et al., 1974) maintain that the various knowledge sources are called upon sequentially, and no meaning can be derived until near the end of an utterance. The present study will assume a fairly weak form of a Marslen-Wilson and Tyler type model.

Reaction time measurement has been the favoured paradigm for investigating the processes of word recognition under different conditions of predictability from word frequency, syntax or semantics. For example, Morton and Long (1976) tested the ability of listeners to detect individual speech sounds embedded in various sentences. They found that reaction times to the phonemes, which were always at the start of words, were around 80 ms faster when the word carrying the phoneme had a high transitional probability, that is, it was easily predictable from prior context. A similar approach was adopted by Cole and Jakimik (1978), in experiments in which listeners were required to detect mispronunciations of words, such as 'pranch' instead of 'branch', and 'ped' instead of 'bed'. Such mispronunciations are thought to be detected when the listener identifies the intended word and spots the acoustic mismatch. The fact that mispronunciations were detected over 150 ms faster when the target word was of high transitional probability indicated the on-line use of the contextual information carried in the sentence.

However, the validity of the phoneme-monitoring task, and to an extent, the mispronunciation-spotting task, rests on the assumption that during the course of normal speech processing and word recognition, phonemes are necessarily extracted from the speech signal. Not only is this assumption contentious, (Fowler et al., 1980), but also these tasks, particularly the former, are not particularly easy for subjects to carry out. More valid paradigms do exist, and one such was used by Marslen-Wilson and Welsh (1978) to tackle the question of the role of context in word recognition. In a monitoring task, the degree of contextual information provided to listeners was stringently controlled, and the stimulus material consisted of correctly pronounced words. The words to be detected by listeners were embedded in short sentences. Three types of sentences were used, these were either syntactically and semantically normal, or contained syntactic and/or semantic anomalies. In addition, some subjects were primed with a context-setting sentence, in order to provide more a priori semantic information. It was found that when the context-setting sentence was present, words could be monitored 50-60 ms faster in normal sentences than in the anomalous sentences right from the beginning of the test sentence. In the absence of the context-setting sentence, the difference was only observed for target words occurring later on in the test sentence. The results thus show that words are most readily identified by listeners when syntactic and semantic information is in evidence, and when the target words occur late in the sentence, such that they are at least partially predictable on the basis of earlier items. A comparable result was obtained by Pisoni and Hunnicut (1981) using a memory task in which listeners were required to remember sentences that were either meaningful or semantically anomalous. Based on percentage memory scores, they discovered an interaction between sentence type and speech type, due to the greater reliance on acoustic information in comprehending the anomalous sentences, and the lesser availability of this information in the synthetic speech.

4.1.2. Applying Word-monitoring to Studies of Synthetic Speech

All the studies of the perception of synthetic speech suggest that, relative to natural speech, it is an impoverished signal, providing fewer acoustic cues to phonetic segments, and so requiring for its comprehension more effort on the part of the listener. It has been established that the context in which speech occurs plays a significant part in the process of word recognition, and it is clear that, owing to its lesser acoustic quality, the reliance on contextual information might be greater for synthetic speech than for its natural counterpart.

It has been shown that there is some uncertainty surrounding studies of synthetic speech which use memory scores as an index of the cognitive effort of speech processing. Firstly, it is difficult to be sure whether subjects are allocating priority to encoding or to rehearsal of the to-be-remembered items, or even whether such a distinction is valid in assessing the intelligibility of a continuous, meaningful speech stream. Secondly, the way that the quality of the speech (synthetic or natural) interacts with the allocation of processing resources seems, from the above studies, to be a function of the type of material used, i.e. whether it is sentences or word lists. Thirdly, that the task necessarily measures subjects' memory for the stimuli *after* the requisite processing has taken place precludes any detailed analysis of temporal aspects of the word recognition process. Such analyses are important to an understanding of the reason for the lower intelligibility of synthetic speech.

Because memory scores are inadequate for the present purpose, and bearing in mind previous work which has demonstrated the feasibility of reaction time for measuring the difficulty of the speech understanding process, it was intended in the present study to use word-monitoring latency to infer the degree of processing effort required by different speech types. Borrowing the paradigm of Marslen-Wilson and Tyler (1980), it was intended to manipulate the degree of contextual information available to listeners, and to observe the way in which this interacted with their ability to recognise words spoken in natural, systematically degraded, and synthetic speech.

It was hoped that the use of word-monitoring latencies in this way would thus provide two things. Firstly, that it would indicate which stage(s) in the process of word recognition is (are) most affected by the quality of the speech input, and how this relates to the way in which listeners make use of syntactic and semantic information throughout the course of a sentence. Secondly, it was hoped that word-monitoring latency would prove to be a sufficiently valid, reliable and sensitive metric to be able to serve as a much needed index of the intelligibility of synthetic speech, thus potentially enabling meaningful comparisons to be made amongst the intelligibility of various speech synthesisers.

4.2. THE WORD-MONITORING TASK

4.2.1. Experimental Details

Subjects
  48 subjects, 24 male and 24 female, were drawn from the British Telecom Human Factors subject panel. No hearing defects were reported by subjects at the time of the experiment. None had had any significant exposure to synthetic speech, nor to word-

monitoring tasks.

Materials

Sixteen meaningful and sixteen nonsense sentences were used as stimulus material. These are listed in an appendix to this chapter. The meaningful sentences each contained 8 'content' words, which were the words to be monitored for: nouns, adjectives, or the past tense of verbs. The median word frequency in both the nonsense and the meaningful sentences was in excess of 100 per million words (Thorndike & Lorge, 1944). The nonsense sentences had the same syntactic structure as the meaningful sentences, but the choice of content words was randomised amongst the sentences, so that the semantic information was effectively removed. The synthetic voice was provided by an *Interstate Electronics 'Prose 2000'* text-to-speech synthesiser. The natural voice was that of a male speaker with 'received pronunciation', speaking at 160 words per minute, the same rate as the default rate of the synthesiser. The talker did not know the purpose of the experiment, nor which words were due to be monitored for. A third tape was constructed by re-recording the natural speech tape, but low-pass filtering it at 1.5 kHz. All recordings were made on high quality tape on a *Ferrograph* reel-to-reel tape recorder, and played to subjects over a high fidelity loudspeaker. As the bandwidth of the speech synthesiser was nominally 0-5 kHz, all recordings were low-pass filtered at 5 kHz as they were played to listeners. Reaction times were measured using a millisecond timer, which started in response to a 1 kHz tone on the second channel of the tape, and which stopped as the subject indicated his/her response using a single microswitch. The location of the trigger tones, and therefore the reaction time measurements, were accurate to within ± 5 ms. All measurements concerning the location of trigger tones and the duration of words were derived from spectrograms made on a *Kay 7800* digital spectrograph.

Procedure

Subjects were given a standard set of instructions, which varied slightly according to the experimental condition. The to-be-monitored words were given to the subjects on cards, only one of which was visible at a time. Subjects were played a short (10 s) passage of the speech they were about to hear and were asked to adjust the volume to a comfortable level whilst listening to this passage. They were then required to listen for the stimulus word in each of the tape-recorded sentences, upon hearing the word to press the response button, then go on to the next card and sentence. They were given no knowledge of results, and were encouraged to respond quickly. They were also warned, where applicable, that the speech they were due to hear would be strange, and/or that the sentences they were about to hear would not make sense.

Design

There were three factors in the study: between-subjects, the *speech type* was either natural, degraded or synthetic; within-subjects, *sentence type* was either nonsense or meaningful and *word position*, i.e. the position in the sentence of the to-be-monitored content word, took a value from 1 to 8. The order of sentence types and the order of sentences within each type (16-1 or 1-16) was counterbalanced. The position within a sentence of the to-be-monitored word was randomised between sentences, with the constraint that each word position occurred twice in each 16-sentence set.

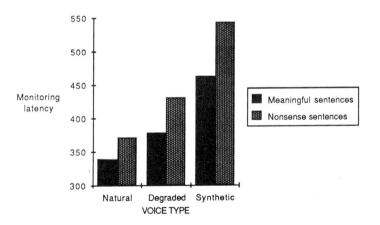

Figure 4.1 - Overall Monitoring Latencies

4.3. RESULTS

Data were analysed using a three-way ANOVA on the SAS statistical package (Cody & Smith, 1984). The main effect of speech type was significant ($F_{(2, 45)}$ = 26.7; $p < 0.0001$) (see Figure 4.1) as were the main effects of memory condition ($F_{(1, 45)}$ = 37.3; $p < 0.0001$) and word position ($F_{(7, 315)}$ = 18.3; $p < 0.0001$) (see Figure 4.2). Table 4.1 shows the mean monitoring latencies for each group. The mean latencies for targets at each word position are appended. The two-way interaction with speech type and memory condition just reached significance ($F_{(2,45)}$ = 3.7; $p < 0.05$). The two-way interaction with memory condition and word position was also significant ($F_{(7, 308)}$ = 24.8; $p < 0.0001$), as was the three-way interaction with speech type, memory condition and word position ($F_{(14, 308)}$ = 4.56; $p < 0.0001$). However, the rather erratic pattern of the word position effect, with considerable departure from a smooth linear or exponential curve, complicates an analysis of the significance of this effect (see Figure 4.3). Therefore the data were re-analysed in terms of the half of the sentence (first or second) in which the target word occurred (see Figure 4.4). These data are shown in Table 4.2. Analysing the word position effect in this way confirmed that the earliness or lateness in the sentence of the target word did affect monitoring latency in the predicted manner. Sentence half had a significant effect ($F_{(1, 45)}$ = 40.04; $p < 0.0001$). The interaction with speech type and sentence half was significant ($F_{(2, 45)}$ = 4.05; $p < 0.05$), as were the interactions with memory condition and sentence half ($F_{(1, 45)}$ = 18.27; $p < 0.0001$), and with speech type, memory condition and sentence half ($F_{(2, 45)}$ = 12.31; $p < 0.0001$).

4.4. DISCUSSION

4.4.1. Semantic Content and Speech Type

The main effect of speech type is not surprising. It is predictable that words could be monitored more readily in the natural speech than in the degraded or synthetic speech. This result is indicative of the different levels of quality or intelligibility of the three speech types: the natural speech being the highest quality, the degraded speech being of lower quality, and the synthetic speech being the lowest quality.

The effect on monitoring latencies of the memory condition, or level of contextual information, indicates the facilitatory effect of semantic information on listeners' ability to recognise the target words. In terms of a Marslen-Wilson type model of word recognition, when monitoring words in meaningful sentences the listener can be said to be activating a 'Word-initial cohort', a number of possible word candidates on the basis of the early acoustic and/or phonetic information in the speech signal, and to be simultaneously rejecting those word

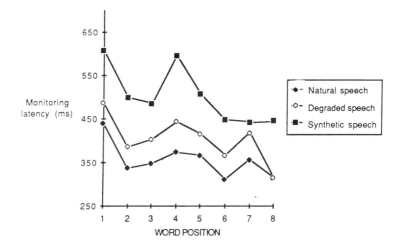

Figure 4.2 - Effect of Word Position
(Mean across Sentence Types)

candidates which do not accord with the current semantic and syntactic context. When monitoring nonsense sentences, in which the
semantic content has been removed, but the syntactic structure
remains, the listener has less information on which to base his or her
judgement of which word candidates to reject. Thus, the decision has
to be deferred until later on in the word, after more acoustic and/or
phonetic input has been processed. Deferring the decision as to the
word's identity gives rise to the greater monitoring latency.

The interaction with memory condition and speech type indicates that the lower the quality of the speech in which sentences are spoken, the greater is the increase in word recognition time when the semantic content of the sentences is removed. This can be explained in similar terms to the above. If the removal of a sentence's semantic content causes the decision as to the identity of a word to be deferred until later on in that word, then that decision must be awaiting the outcome of further acoustic and/or phonetic analysis (possibly in interaction with syntactic analysis, although this is not the limiting factor). When the acoustic stream less accurately specifies what phonemes and/or syllables are intended, then clearly the necessary analysis will proceed more slowly. In other words, low quality speech leads to difficulty in extracting phonetic information, which leads to longer word-recognition time.

This explanation can be illustrated by reference to the durations of the words that were monitored for in the test sentences. Taking the case of the natural speech, the mean monitoring latency for words embedded in meaningful sentences was 339 ms. The mean duration of the these words was 390 ms. If the listener's response execution time[1] is taken to be of the order of 50-75 ms (Marslen-Wilson & Tyler, 1980), this means that the listener has recognised the word, with the aid of the semantic content of the sentence, around 277 ms after its onset (or after 71% of the word has been heard). Compare this with the words in the nonsense sentences, which had a mean duration of 300 ms,[2] and for which the mean monitoring latency was 371 ms. These words could be said to be recognised on average 308 ms after their onset, that is, 8 ms after they have finished. So for samples of

Table 4.1. Mean Monitoring Latencies (ms)

	SPEECH TYPE			
	Natural	Degraded	Synthetic	Mean
CONTEXT LEVEL				
Meaningful	339	377	463	393
Nonsense	371	430	544	448
Mean	355	404	504	421

[1] Response execution time being the time between the events of the listener recognising the word and of actually indicating a response.

[2] The difference in word lengths between the nonsense and meaningful sentences does not damage the claims here. In the nonsense sentences the shorter duration of the average word means that all the acoustic information carried by that word arrives earlier, and hence it is uniquely specified (in the acoustic domain) more quickly than the average word in the meaningful sentences. Were the mean word durations to be made equal in both sentence types, the reported effects would be accentuated.

natural speech, the absence of semantic content in an otherwise syntactically appropriate sentence lengthens the mean word recognition
time by around 32 ms. This same amount of analysis takes 53 ms for
degraded speech (mean word length 390 ms for meaningful sentences,
300 ms for nonsense sentences), and 81 ms for synthetic speech
(mean word length 405 ms for meaningful sentences, 329 ms for nonsense sentences).

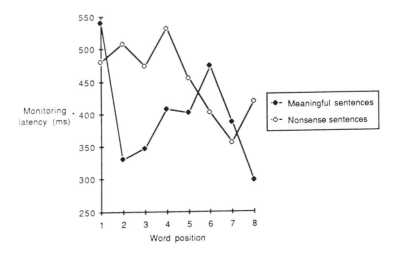

Figure 4.3 - Word Position Effect (Mean across Voice Types)

4.4.2. The Effect on Word Recognition of Word Position

The significant effect of the target word occurring at different locations in the test sentence is shown in Figure 4.2. This shows how monitoring latency gradually decreases as the target occurs later on in the sentence. This is due to the derivation by the listener of the syntactic structure of the sentence. As the sentence progresses, so the structural constraints on the identity of words become stronger; more structural information is available to the listener on which to base his or her judgement of which word has occurred, and hence recognition can occur earlier on in the target word. Finer features of the word position curves are difficult to interpret owing to their irregular shape: the words occurring at some word positions have characteristics which introduce a large amount of variance into the results. Some of these differences are due to suprasegmental features, which are discussed below. However, other characteristics are affecting the time taken to recognise certain words. Word frequency was balanced within sentences and across sentence types, so this is not affecting results. The number of syllables making up each word may be affecting some recognition latencies and hence some word positions. The varying lengths of words will also be causing differences in the time taken to recognise them (the information as to the acoustic structure of short words obviously arrives earlier after the word's onset than it would in a long word). These factors do not necessarily damage the claims made regarding differences between meaningful and nonsense sentences (within a particular speech type). Nor does it damage the claims regarding the differences amongst the speech types on the whole. They do, however, preclude any detailed analysis of the trends in the word position effect for *individual* speech types or memory conditions.

Figure 4.4 illustrates the word position data when reconsidered in terms of whether the target occurred in the first or second half of the sentence. This shows the significant interaction with speech type and sentence half. The explanation for this is by now familiar, assuming

Table 4.2. Monitoring Latencies by List Half (ms).

	Meaningful Sentences		Nonsense Sentences	
	1st half	2nd half	1st half	2nd half
SPEECH TYPE				
Natural	352	326	395	347
Degraded	399	356	459	401
Synthetic	469	458	641	461
Mean	407	380	498	403

that knowledge of the sentence's syntactic structure assists word recognition decisions in a similar way to knowledge of its semantic content. [3] Where syntactic information can be used to aid the decision of which of the initially-activated word candidates to reject, that decision is made more quickly, and monitoring latencies are consequently shorter. When targets occur early on in the sentence and little exists in the way of syntactic constraints, then there is more reliance on an analysis of the word's acoustic-phonetic structure. For lower quality speech, this structure is less rich in phonetic information, so the analysis is less effective in defining the word's possible identity. Thus, sufficient analysis takes longer, and longer monitoring latencies result.

The interaction with memory condition and sentence half suggests a difference in the extent to which the syntactic structure can be derived in the two sentence types. In meaningful sentences, the syntactic structure and the semantic content are mutually supportive: knowing what the sentence means helps the listener to infer what class of word is likely to occur next. This means that the syntactic frame or 'shape' of the sentence is available to the listener quite early on in the sentence. This contrasts with the nonsense sentences, where the syntactic structure is not made available to the listener until much later on in the sentence, and so the to-be-monitored words in the second half are recognised considerably faster (the recognition decision being aided by syntactic constraints) than those in the first half. The third interaction here, that with speech type, memory condition and sentence half, is again indicative of the lower quality speech samples containing less phonetic information per unit time. Where word-monitoring has to be carried out with the minimal assistance from syntactic and semantic constraints, that is, in the first half of a nonsense sentence, then the quality of the speech signal is most likely to affect the latency of word recognition. In these cases, the greatest difference is observed amongst the three speech types. Conversely, as the low-level acoustic analysis comes to form a smaller part of the overall analysis, ultimately in the second half of a meaningful sentence, then the type of speech in which the word is spoken becomes less important and affects recognition latency less.

Returning to the characteristics of the word position effects illustrated in Figure 4.2, it is interesting to consider further some of the possible reasons for the many fluctuations in the curves. A salient feature of these effects is that, whereas the curves for natural and for degraded speech are virtually parallel, the curve for the synthetic speech,

---

[3] Marslen Wilson and Tyler (1980) claim that semantic constraints are almost twice as effective as syntactic constraints in speeding response time. However, they also note that '..there is nothing in the data to compel a distinction between semantic and interpretative (syntactic) knowledge sources' (p. 60).

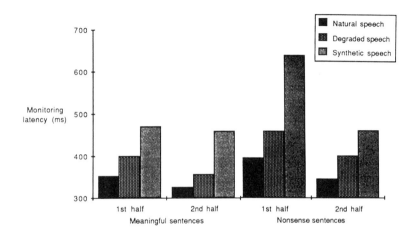

Figure 4.4 - Effect of Word Position (by List Half)

although it is also very roughly exponential, shows certain unique characteristics. Bearing in mind that the only difference between the natural and the degraded speech was that the latter was a low-pass filtered version of the former, it is likely that the reason for the perceived lower quality of the synthetic speech is not merely that individual words are inaccurately specified in the frequency domain. The ways in which the synthetic speech differs from the other two samples is likely to be due to inaccuracies in the specification of units larger than a word. What this means is that some contribution to the greater monitoring latency for the synthetic words is made by the inappropriateness of the stress and intonation patterns. For example, it has been established that stressed syllables are more perceptible than unstressed syllables (Cutler & Foss, 1977), and this may bring about changes in the word position effects if the stress-assignment algorithm used by the synthesiser is inaccurate and/or too generalised. For example, it may stress *all* content words, or always stress nouns more than verbs without taking sufficient account of the positions of these words within a sentence. Inappropriately stressed words will therefore be made easier to recognise (and so quicker to monitor), while the monitoring latencies for inappropriately unstressed words will be increased. This will cause spurious within-sentence variations which cannot be explained by reference just to within-word features.

Another example of suprasegmental differences which may give rise to anomalies in the word position effect is the shape of the intonation contours. Not only do changes in the fundamental frequency (F0) of a sample at a *word* level provide clues as to the identity the phonetic segments therein (Haggard et al., 1970), but also sentence level rises and falls in F0 serve to direct attention towards and away from particular parts of the sentence. If the way that such variations are executed by the synthesiser differs from that of the human speaker used here, then differences in the word position effects will result. That the pitch contour of the Prose 2000 synthesiser does have some effect in helping listeners recognise words has been demonstrated by Slowiaczek and Nusbaum (1985), although they point out that perception of the segmental information is more critical than this to the intelligibility of the speech. However, they only compared the Prose 2000 speaking with default pitch contour to the same synthesiser speaking with a monotone pitch pattern, and although this does show that some intonation is better than none, it does not highlight the specific weaknesses of the contour adopted by the synthesiser. [4] A more rigorous analysis of these effects than is possible here would need to consider the effects on word recognition latency of the inherent differences between the intonation contours in the natural and the synthetic speech. Such an analysis would be informed by considering the correlation (if any) between the height of F0 in the monitored words and the recognition latency for those words.

4.4.3. An Index of Speech Intelligibility

A definition of intelligibility in terms of word recognition latencies and the knowledge sources involved in the word recognition process provides a good foundation for a metric which can be used to indicate the intelligibility of different forms of speech. However, such a

---

[4] In fact, statements are normally spoken with an average *fall* in pitch from their start to their finish. Thus, using a sentence with a monotone pitch actually represents an effective pitch *rise* across the sentence, and thus makes it an inadequate control condition.

metric, in addition to the criteria mentioned earlier, should not simply reflect features of the test material from which its value is derived. To this end, it is desirable to express the recognition latencies either in ratio form (perhaps the proportion of the word which needs to be heard before recognition can take place), or else in terms of the changes in recognition latency resulting from alterations in the sentences' structure. Executing changes in the syntactic structure of sentences is one possibility, but apart from completely removing the syntactic form (by creating random word orders), it is difficult to know how to execute *controlled* changes that would bring about predictable effects. It is proposed, then, that the increase in recognition latency resulting from the removal of a sentence's semantic content would serve the desired purpose. In the present study, the values obtained for this measure were 32 ms for natural speech, 53 ms for degraded speech, and 81 ms for synthetic speech. That the changes in this value reflect changes in the speed of carrying out a known amount of processing, at a known level of analysis, means that the figure for natural speech can usefully be considered as a baseline against which to compare the quality or intelligibility of the other two samples. For the sake of convenience, this proposed metric will be referred to as the 'Increase in Recognition Latency for Nonsense Words' or IRLNW. There are a number of reasons why IRLNW is particularly suitable as a speech quality metric, not least because it satisfies many of the criteria for a good intelligibility metric mentioned earlier.

Firstly, when comparing the different speech types, that the differences in the lengths of time taken to carry out exactly the same amount of processing were found to be significantly different implies that the metric is sufficiently *sensitive*. Had the differences in IRLNW been only slight in the present study, this would tend to detract from its usefulness. It is significant that the speech samples used in the study were actually comprehensible to virtually all listeners, and this indicates that IRLNW can be claimed to do more than just discriminate between intelligible and unintelligible forms of speech: it can enumerate differing *degrees* of intelligibility. Secondly, IRLNW is a *valid* index of speech quality. Normal, everyday speech understanding is necessarily reliant on the process of word recognition. The harder it is to carry out that process, or the longer it takes, the more difficult must the speech be to understand. IRLNW indicates the difficulty of that process. An approach such as this is in stark contrast to metrics which rely on subjective judgements of speech intelligibility or speech processing effort (e.g. CCITT, 1980). That speech understanding is carried out so effortlessly by human listeners suggests that such judgements of listening effort would be very difficult to make, would have little validity, and would be more sensitive to range effects and subjective preferences than to actual differences in objective speech quality (Bennett & Lincoln, 1985). Thirdly, IRLNW is a more *parsimonious* metric than any of those previously proposed. All it assumes is that words spoken in lower quality speech require for their recognition that more analysis be carried out on their acoustic structure. It does not need to assume anything about the units by which word recognition is carried out, whether they are phonemes, syllables, features, etc. Neither is it reliant on listeners' memory for the speech samples, and so does not have to assume anything about whether processing resources are being allocated to encoding, rehearsal or retrieval of the items.

4.5. CONCLUSIONS

(1)   It has been shown in this study that when subjects have to identify words in a continuous speech stream, the speed at which this can be done is proportional to the intelligibility of that speech. However, in interpreting this conclusion, there is a danger of becoming involved in a circular definition of intelligibility (high quality speech causes lower monitoring latencies, and so must be more intelligible... etc.), unless some attempt is made to define the reasons for the observed effect. What has been pointed out is that the low quality speech is less rich in phonetic information, and so makes more difficult the task of deriving the segments (phonemes, syllables, etc.) upon which lexical access is based. An analogy with the visual presentation of words would exist in the case of a poor photocopy of a page of writing, or of a page of untidy handwriting. Although the visual stimuli (auditory in the case of speech) are all present in some form, they less accurately specify which letters (phonemes or syllables etc. for speech) are intended by the writer (speaker), and so preliminary analyses of the stimuli are made more difficult and hence slower.

(2)   The increase in word recognition latency when a sentence's context is removed provides a figure which forms the basis of an appropriate metric for speech intelligibility. Such a metric is sensitive to subtle changes in the objective quality of the speech, is valid in its particular application, relies on a parsimonious model of word recognition, and avoids many of the pitfalls of either subjective ratings of speech quality and listening effort, or listening tests involving memory performance.

(3)   The samples of speech compared in this study were shown to be significantly different when rated with the above metric. The reasons for the differences at a word level have been mentioned, but some of the reason for the lower quality of the synthetic speech has been speculated to be its inaccurate or inappropriate application of stress and intonation.

(4)   Future work should concentrate on the following questions:

(a) What is the correlation between F0 in the monitored words and the latency with which they are monitored, and does this suggest that the intelligibility of synthetic speech can be significantly improved through more accurate intonation algorithms?

(b) What are the specific differences at a word level between high and low quality speech, especially natural and synthetic speech, which give the observed effects ? This question could be considered from many angles. If it was hypothesised that differences were mainly in the frequency domain, spectrographic analysis of the two types of words would be appropriate. If it was thought to be the case that the indeterminate phonetic content of synthetic words caused the activation of so many possible word candidates that it was their elimination which consumed the additional recognition time, then a comparison of the 'word-initial cohort' activated by the same words in the two types of speech would be appropriate. Thirdly, if the differences in the quality of the two speech types was thought to be attributable to different amounts of experience of listening to the two, then an examination of the changes in word-monitoring latency with the extent of such experience would be a suitable test of this hypothesis.

(c) Is word-monitoring latency, or the increase in this due to the removal of a sentence's contextual information, a *reliable* indicator of speech intelligibility ? To answer this would require a re-test of the current speech types using different listeners and materials, and also possibly a series of replications of the test on samples of speech degraded along a particular continuum (e.g. decreasing the cut-off point for low-pass filtering, increasing the signal-to-noise ratio, decreasing the sampling rate while distorting the speech through quantisation).

4.6. APPENDIX TO CHAPTER 4

4.6.1. Monitoring Latencies for Each Word Position

(i) Meaningful sentences:

	Word Position							
	1	2	3	4	5	6	7	8
VOICE TYPE								
Natural	472	263	333	338	319	301	417	267
Degraded	512	329	345	409	373	348	448	256
Synthetic	636	400	367	473	513	450	498	370
Mean	540	331	348	407	401	473	387	298

(ii) Nonsense sentences:

	Word position							
	1	2	3	4	5	6	7.	8
VOICE TYPE								
Natural	404	408	360	407	412	319	295	360
Degraded	460	440	461	475	455	385	388	375
Synthetic	576	672	601	714	499	442	385	518
Mean	480	507	474	532	455	401	356	418

4.6.2. Sentences Used for Word Monitoring Task

(a) Nonsense sentences

1. The first visitor slammed her nervous path to the nearest fresh gates.
2. The five women passed to a brown silence near the south room on the flag.
3. The big new station poured the building and was the top smoke.
4. The iron place turned the storey under the meal and cut at her long train.
5. People read at the cave and looked for white shutters and thick captives.
6. A narrow town rushed on his bright rain and his wife started her river.
7. The vegetables stood off small main boats and hid them for his three ducks.
8. The street opened from the bowl, asked the chickens, and felt the latest corner.
9. A green jar and a glass jar drove on the noisy boy in the corner.
10. The outlaws worried their sweets to the young runners and called

a large man.
11. The painter frightened the heavy blue picture and hurried up the hidden hand.
12. The stupid brother hit through the fruit and closed the table and book in the cage.
13. The butcher worked the new girl, who prepared that the light led four.
14. The customer stared at the short house as it fell from the black doors of the afternoon.
15. The woman wrapped younger and hot, but old chops shone in the afternoon.
16. The red farm ran through the sunny shelf and day of the narrow storey.

(b) Meaningful sentences

1. The young woman drove her new car to the nearest main town.
2. The iron gates led to a short path near the three boats on the river.
3. A long white hand opened the window and closed the brown shutters.
4. The stupid girl hid the sweets under the table and looked at her younger brother.
5. People called at the farm and asked for fresh fruit and green vegetables.
6. An old painter worked on his latest picture and his wife read her book.
7. The butcher cut off five thick chops and wrapped them for his new customer.
8. The boy ran from the room, slammed the door, and hit the nervous visitor.
9. A blue bowl and a glass jar stood on the the small shelf in the corner.
10. The outlaws hurried their captives to the hidden cave and prepared a large meal.
11. The runners passed the first red flag and turned up the narrow street.
12. The noisy train rushed through the station and frightened the ducks and chickens in the cage.
13. The silence worried the four women, who felt that the place was dangerous.
14. The man stared at the black smoke as it poured from the top storey of the building.
15. The day started hot and sunny, but heavy rain fell in the afternoon.
16. The bright light shone through the south windows and doors of the large house.

5

Human Speech Production and Automatic Speech Recognition:

Resolving some Differences

M. Talbot

5.1. EXISTING SPEECH RECOGNITION DEVICES

5.1.1. Some Problems

Automatic speech recognition (ASR) is becoming in some applications a valuable enhancement to the man-machine interface (Talbot, 1985). The particular advantages of using speech to communicate with machines are well documented, and in some cases, such as in the use of ASR in aids for the disabled, are considerable (Damper, 1984). However, the full potential of ASR is at present not being realised: recognition rates are unacceptably low, and speech recognisers with reasonably large vocabularies need individualised sets of voice templates, so that every potential user has to 'train' the device by providing voice samples before being able to use the recogniser. There are exceptions to the template-matching approach, however. A new generation of speech recognisers is about to become commercially available, which is based on the recognition of the phonemes of which words are composed rather than the words themselves. These 'Phonetic Recognisers' do not require a lengthy training phase, as the speaker needs only to provide samples of each phoneme to be recognised, not each word. Such systems also have the potential for an unlimited vocabulary.

The capabilities of template-matching speech recognisers appear to have levelled out over the past three or four years, and thus this method appears to be performing as well as it ever will. Until phonetic recognition becomes more widely available, any significant improvements in the quality and level of performance of ASR systems are likely to come about as a result of improving aspects of the speech *interface* rather than the hardware itself. Specifically, such improvements would take account of features of the voice of the user and the way in which he or she talks to the speech recogniser.

Existing ASR devices, claim their manufacturers, can recognise isolated utterances under controlled conditions with between 95% and 100% success. The 'recognition' referred to is the proportion of occasions on which the device compares spectral analyses of unknown utterances to the array of voice templates, and comes up with the correct match. A particular utterance will only be recognised if the degree of similarity with its stored template reaches a pre-defined criterion. There are two distinct ways in which this recognition process may fail:

(1)   the utterance may be badly matched, that is, matched to the wrong template, or

(2)   it may fail to reach the criterion for similarity with any of the templates, and will not be matched at all.

5.1.2. Some Possible Solutions

The number of bad matches (or substitutions) can be reduced by keeping the number of words in the system's vocabulary to the minimum required by the task, and also by ensuring that the chosen words are acoustically dissimilar. However, the second type of recognition error, misses, are clearly a consequence of a change having taken place in the user's diction between the time of training the device and of actually using it, and so need to be dealt with by some method which tracks this change over time.

Regarding the training phase, this conventionally consists of reading aloud the list of words which are to be subsequently recognised. Each word is read several times (four, for example) and a template is made as a composite of the repetitions. Thus, each template is supposed to represent the 'average' utterance of the word to which it corresponds. This list-reading technique leaves much to be desired, however. The monotony of having to read the same list over several times is reflected in the readers' intonation: they will speak in a dull, flat voice which is not reproduced during the execution of the actual task. As regards the effect of the task on diction, there are a number of factors which are likely to affect the user in such a way that his or her pronunciation of the permitted words is altered. Recognition errors themselves may cause the user to lose confidence in the system, and this has been observed to affect diction such that recognition accuracy will be reduced even further (Martin & Welch, 1980). Similarly, the users' emotional state may be affected by the performance of the system during execution of the task. They may, for example, become frustrated or angry if the error rate is high, or may become relaxed if this is particularly low, they may also become stressed by the pace of the recognition process, or fatigued if the task takes too long or the response time of the system is too great. Again, these factors are likely to affect the 'task' voice.

Thus, with the aim of maximising the proportion of successful word recognitions, there are two goals which need to be achieved through efficient design of the speech interface. Firstly, the templates for each word need to constitute accurate examples of how those words are normally uttered by the speaker. Secondly, the templates should be treated such that, throughout the course of the speech recognition task, they do not become out of date if the speaker's diction changes as a consequence of task demands, levels of motivation, or the passage of time.

It is because of the considerable differences between human speech production and automatic speech recognition that these elements of adaptation are necessary. Speech recognition, as described, is attempted on the basis of a representation of the talker's voice which is set up once only by the recogniser, and not altered. The to-be-recognised voice, however, cannot be adequately represented by a once-off sample (even if this sample is a composite of several training passes), and is also constantly changing.

There have been few previous attempts to have the speech recognition system adapt to the talker, and so the onus in overcoming poor recognition rates has been on the talker, who has had to adapt to the needs of the system. This adaptation is considerable, and its extent generally depends on the amount of experience of the talker. It is clear that users who are experienced in operating speech recognisers are able to achieve significantly better recognition rates than are naive users, presumably owing to the former's more sophisticated conceptual model of the recognition process. They are able to maintain the required uniformity of pronunciation during training and task execution, and to maintain optimal or near-optimal levels of volume and emphasis. On the other hand, the author's experience is that people unfamiliar with speech recognition systems have a much less accurate model of the process: they will attempt to improve poor recognition rates by speaking more slowly and at a lower than normal pitch, as though they were communicating over a poor telephone line. However, Underwood (1980) notes how the main strategy he has observed being used by naive users is to speak more loudly. None of these strategies would be likely to significantly improve the performance of the majority of recognisers.

Two adverse factors, from the point of view of the system adapting to the needs of the talker, have been identified as: the monotony that is inevitably induced in a speaker's voice during list-reading as a method of training a speech recogniser; and the variability produced in that voice during performance of a task using the recogniser. The rest of this paper considers how adaptation might alleviate these problems, and also describes an evaluation of a proposed adaptive speech interface which incorporates some of the solutions proposed above.

5.2. PREVIOUS WORK

Thus, the first feature of the adaptive speech interface should be a means of avoiding monotony during training. The following are some examples of schemes which have been designed to do this.

Conolly (1977) advocated randomising the order in which the word list is read during training, in order to achieve a wide variety of articulatory environments and to remove the predictability of the words, such that the rhythmic patterning inherent in reading lists of words would be reduced. DeGeorge (1981) found that, at least for naive users, reading the word list sequentially and repeating it as required is preferable to repetitive training, whereby each word is repeated the requisite number of times before going on to the next one. Green, et al. (1983) described a possible task-like training phase, in which aspects of the speech recognition task are imitated whilst the templates are being collected; they do not implement or evaluate this, however. This method would seem to tackle most directly the problem of differing contexts at the time of training and of task execution. To surreptitiously train the device whilst imitating the task itself would be likely to result in a library of particularly representative templates.

The second feature of the adaptive speech interface should be adaptation to drifts in the speaker's voice during task execution. Green et al. (1983) tackled this problem by using a scheme of updating the templates according to the changing characteristics of the user's voice. This scheme consisted of constantly averaging the characteristics of a template for a given word with the characteristics of the current pronunciation of that word. This resulted, in effect, in constantly retraining the recogniser. For example, if a certain utterance was made, and was recognised to be the word 'left', then one of the templates for 'left' would then be updated in accordance with how 'left' was just pronounced. The danger here, of course, is that if the utterance had not in fact been 'left', and a bad match had actually occurred, then the updating process would corrupt the matched template.

One way of avoiding this erroneous updating would be to provide an error signal indicating when the match is good or bad (i.e correct or incorrect recognition), so that on no occasion will a template be updated by averaging it with the current pronunciation of that word.

Green et al. employed their updating scheme using such an error signal, as provided by the experimenter. Thus, each time an utterance was made, the experimenter indicated by the press of a button whether it had been correctly or incorrectly recognised. Only in the event of a correct recognition did template updating take place. This scheme, using an external error signal, was successful to the extent of improving the recognition rate on a four-word vocabulary from 70% to 89%. An external error signal was also used as part of the criterion for template updating in a study by Damper and McDonald (1984). They in fact used two criteria: if the input utterance and the template to which it was matched were sufficiently similar, and the correct word was recognised (i.e. template and utterance belonged to the same 'class'), then the matched template would be updated. The requisite degree of similarity could be set by the experimenters, and the way in which the word was verified as correctly recognised was by the speaker making a 'yes' or 'no' response to the recogniser's selection. Damper and McDonald achieved a 4% reduction in error rates due to their adaptive system, although only one experimental subject was tested.

So, it is possible to incorporate an element of adaptation into a speech recognition algorithm. However, it is desirable that this adaptation should not have to rely on an external error signal to indicate whether or not an utterance has just been correctly recognised (as in the Damper and McDonald case), but rather that this error signal should be internally generated. Green et al. (1983) tried such a system, in which correct recognition was, in effect, signalled internally.

They increased the number of templates stored by the recogniser, and located them in different 'vocabularies'. Only if an utterance was recognised as being the same word, at a strict matching criterion, on two separate vocabularies, was one of the templates for that word (a different one) updated in line with the current utterance. In terms of a control system analogy, they claimed their system to be stable, in that the criterion for updating was strict, and damped, in that the large number of templates present ensured that the detrimental effect of incorrectly updating any one of them was minimised.

Green et al. observed an improvement in recognition rate, due to their 'continuous updating', from 70% to 88% correct recognitions. However, the former figure was the recognition rate obtained using a non-adaptive system and just one vocabulary of templates, while the improved figure of 88% was the recognition rate on the adaptive condition (i.e. with updating), but with eight templates for each word (four templates per word on each of two vocabularies). Thus, by introducing the multiple templates, Green et al. also increased the simple probability that a given utterance would find a match some-where amongst the templates, and would thus be recognised. This lessens the likelihood that the improvement in recognition rates was due to updating alone.

5.3. CURRENT EXPERIMENTAL WORK

5.3.1. Introduction

The previous section described ways in which it is possible to make the speech interface adaptive to certain features of human speech, and how these methods have been shown to be effective in improving speech recognition rates. Two things appear to be missing from the studies described: an evaluation of the method of training whereby task-like factors are imitated during template collection; and a rigorous evaluation of the effect of template updating on recognition performance, using an internal error signal, employing a suitable experimental design, and avoiding the facilitative effect of simply increasing the number of templates active within the recogniser. The remainder of this chapter describes some experimental work which has been carried out in an effort to make such an evaluation.

5.3.1.1. Experimental details

64 subjects, male and female, drawn from the British Telecom Human Factors subject panel, were used in the evaluation. The scenario was one in which subjects were required to interrogate a database of train times using an automatic speech recogniser. Information was delivered in synthetic speech, using the Prose 2000 text-to-speech synthesiser. The two factors manipulated during the evaluation were:

(1)   the type of training, either normal list-reading or task-like train-ing; and

(2)   the template treatment, wherein templates were either constantly updated or not altered at all after the initial training phase.

To train the recogniser conventionally, subjects read aloud the list of eight words permitted by the train timetable, three names of destina-tions, 'Filey', 'Margate' and 'Poole'; three days, 'Tuesday', 'Thursday' and 'Weekend', and 'Yes' and 'No'. Each word was repeated eight times. In the task-like training condition, templates were collected surreptitiously whilst the system behaved as though it were actually running the timetable. The sequence of words prompted by the sys-tem during this phase was fixed, so that each question asked of the subject could have only one answer. Thus, the templates were collected in the same order as for the list-reading training phase. The length of the task-like training session and the rate at which questions were asked were identical to that of a typical interaction when actually using the voice-operated timetable. In addition, recognition errors were simulated during the task-like training by occasionally asking the subject to repeat words, with a frequency equal to that of the normally occurring rate of missed utterances.

The number of templates stored, their division into 'vocabularies' and the template updating scheme was exactly the same as that used by Green et al. (1983), in order to re-test their results against a valid control condition (no updating, but the same number of templates). In addition, the same speech recogniser, the Heuristics H2000, was used. The data collected were the number of good and bad matches, and the identity of frequently badly matched words.

5.3.1.2. Results of experiments

Recognition rates of Automatic Speech Recognisers are typically distributed with severe negative skew. Several subjects obtain very good recognition rates, while a long tail of subjects obtain poor or very poor recognition (e.g. Green et al. 1983; Green & Clark, 1981). For this reason, non-parametric techniques of statistical analysis were preferred. Thus, the statistical tests are based on the Chi-squared test for the independence of groups.

Table 5.1 lists the overall percentage of utterances which were missed (unrecognised), badly matched (misrecognised) and correctly matched (recognised) by the recogniser. The recognition rates for males and females were significantly different overall. Males obtained, on average, 12% better recognition ((1)=4.99; $p < 0.05$). The data are broken down into the four conditions and shown in Table 5.2. These data are also illustrated (see Figure 5.1).

Table 5.1. Average Recognition Rates over All Conditions (%)

	Recognised	Unrecognised	Misrecognised
Male:	88.5	7.0	4.5
Female:	76.5	15.75	7.75
Mean:	82.5	11.4	6.1

Table 5.2. Detailed Recognition Figures (%)

	List-reading		Task-like training	
	Updating	No updating	Updating	No updating
Male	86	87	90	91
Female	69	68	87	82
Mean	77.5	77.5	88.5	86.5

For the female subjects, template updating caused a slight but non-significant improvement in recognition rate on the 'list-reading' condition ((1)=0.02) and a greater, but still non-significant improvement in recognition rate on the 'task-like training' condition ((1)=0.95). Updating the templates of the male subjects appeared to depress recognition rate, but the effect is again non-significant on both the 'list-reading' and the 'task-like training' condition ((1)=0.04 and 0.03, respectively). Regarding the effect of training method, there was an increase in recognition rate due to the use of task-like training, for both male and female subjects. This improvement is non-significant for males on both the condition of template updating ((1)=0.76), and on that of no template updating ((1)=0.78). For the female subjects however, the improvement is significant both with updating ((1)=9.44; $p < 0.01$) and without ((1)=5.25; $p < 0.05$).

5.3.2. Discussion: Can ASR be Made to Adapt?

Male voices were recognised significantly more reliably than female voices, with a mean difference of 12%. The means by which templates were trained was found to have a non-significant effect on recognition rates for males, but to significantly improve recognition rates for females. The method of constantly updating the stored templates, which replicated that of Green et al. (1983), was found to have no significant effect on either males' or females' recognition rates. The difference between the sexes' recognition rates is a common feature of ASR performance figures. The reason for it has not been firmly established, but it is thought to be due to the higher pitch of female voices. This causes a wide separation of the spectral lines corresponding to the voice, and a consequent lowering of the resolution with which the formant structure is sampled (e.g. DeGeorge, 1981).

The interaction with sex and training type could be due to a ceiling effect, in that the males' recognition rates were of such a level that task-like training could not improve them. The considerably lower rates observed for females were, however, improved as a result of this method of template collection. Thus, at least for females, this

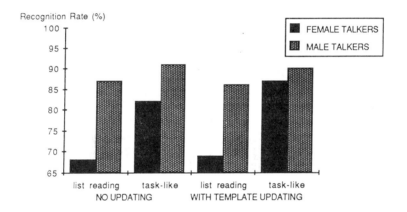

Figure 5.1 - Overall Recognition Rates (%)

confirms the hypothesis that list-reading is an inadequate method of training, and that adapting the training scheme to avoid the monotony of diction that list-reading produces improves the validity of the voice templates.

An alternative explanation for the lack of effect of the adaptive training for the male speakers is that males, regardless of the training type they undergo, always speak similarly both when training and when actually using the recogniser: either they always speak expressively and the list-reading fails to produce a monotonous voice, or else they always speak monotonously and the task-like training fails to make their voice expressive.

The intention of template updating in this study was to prevent the templates becoming out of date through drifts in speakers' diction. Assuming that the task was sufficiently long to produce such drifts, then the present scheme of updating, which replicates exactly that used by Green et al. (1983), is evidently ineffectual. In the light of the fact that Green et al. and Damper and McDonald (1984) were able to demonstrate the efficacy of updating using an external error signal, it may be concluded that the present result is due to the unreliability of the internal error signal. What is needed to create a truly self-adaptive system is some means of generation of such a signal which ensures that the incoming utterance has been correctly matched to a template, and only then to use it to modify that template. What may have been happening in the present study is that occasionally an incoming utterance was erroneously matched with the same template in two separate 'vocabularies', and thus a template was actually *corrupted* rather than improved through updating, thereby putting it out of commission. The failure to replicate Green et al.'s results with the internally generated error signal would indicate that the improvement they observed was due more to the safeguards they made against this effect of erroneous updates, through greatly increasing the number of stored templates, than to the beneficial effect of updating itself.

Future studies, as well as seeking to provide a more veridical error signal, should also vary the degree of similarity between template and utterance which is used as the criterion for deciding whether or not updating should take place. Damper & McDonald found the efficacy of updating to be sensitive to this parameter. In addition, it would be instructional to compare the specific effects of template training and updating regimes with the effect of experience in using a speech recogniser. It is known that people can learn to speak effectively and consistently during recognition, and to provide task-like utterances during training. So, whereas the goal of the present study has been to test methods by which an ASR system may adapt to the speech variations of the user, the results should be considered in the light that it may be more beneficial to train the users to improve recognition rates by adapting to the requirements of the machine.

6

Representing Dialogues for Conversational Interaction

J. A. Waterworth

6.1. INTRODUCTION

This chapter is principally concerned with the way in which strategies for conversational interaction between a human and a machine can be represented in a computer system. The first part of the chapter very briefly outlines a small part of linguistics, Speech Act Theory and related approaches, that have attempted to account for the way in which the meanings of speech or language productions in a particular context are dependent on, and may be interpreted in terms of, that context, i.e. pragmatics. Although only a brief overview is presented here, such considerations are important because of the impact they have on knowledge representation for conversational interaction.

Knowledge representation schemes that can be brought to bear on the problem of modelling and controlling interactive strategies are discussed in the second part of the chapter. Possible criteria for assessing the appropriateness of such schemes are presented, followed by a brief review of the most popular current approaches.

In the third part the focus is on issues of dialogue control and specification. The notion of a discrete dialogue control module for language-based interaction is introduced and discussed, followed by examples of alternative dialogue specification mechanisms and a discussion of their relative merits in terms of such factors as ease of specification (for the dialogue designer) and power.

6.2. SPEECH ACTS AND RELATED LANGUAGE THEORIES

6.2.1. Speech Act Theory

Austin (1962) distinguished two sorts of utterance: performatives, which do things; and constatives, which say things (describe states of affairs). An example of a performative would be "I bet you five pounds". Austin made the claim that although constatives can be true or false, performatives cannot be given truth conditions, they are always true if uttered 'felicitously' - if they conform to certain 'felicity conditions'. If I say "I promise to attend the meeting" to someone who is in a position to accept such a promise (i.e. if felicitously said), I have done something, and it makes no sense to ask if the statement is true or false. But if I say "I hereby declare war on France" I have done nothing, because I do not have the authority to make that statement felicitously. Austin also suggested that constatives can be assessed in the light of their 'felicity'. Felicity conditions, when satisfied, link words and institutional procedures, i.e. performatives are sorts of ceremonies for doing things publicly with words. This view gave rise to a general theory of Speech Acts, made famous by Austin's student Searle (1969), of which constatives are a special case. According to Speech Act Theory, all utterances, in addition to meaning whatever they mean, perform specific actions (they do things) according to their 'force'. Austin identified three ways of doing things with words: locutionary acts, utterances of determinate sense and reference; illocutionary acts, utterances that have their effect by virtue of the conventional 'force' associated with them (promising, declaring, offering, betting, etc. - i.e. explicit performatives); and perlocutionary acts, which are utterances that produce effects on their hearers which are special to the circumstances (the effect of what is done by an utterance, rather than the doing). Speech Acts have come to be associated with illocutionary acts, and with perlocutionary effects.

Searle has become identified with the 'taxonomic approach' to Speech Acts, since he attempted to distinguish the different types of illocutionary force and their felicity conditions. He concluded (Searle, 1976) that there are five, and only five, types of illocutionary act: representatives (committing the speaker to the truth of a statement), directives (trying to get the addressee to do something), commissives (committing the speaker to doing something in the future), expressives (expressing a psychological state, e.g. thanking, apologising), and declarations (changing the state of affairs, usually by appealing to extra-linguistic institutions). This classificatory or taxonomic approach has been criticised in several quarters. Levinson (1983) points out that the classification is not principled, not being based in a systematic way on felicity conditions. The general criticism of the approach rests on doubts about the possibility of identifying and classifying all possible functions of language. But this is not to say that in more restricted circumstances, where the aim is less ambitious (e.g. in the identification and implementation of dialogue strategies for human-computer communication in a limited domain), a taxonomic approach may not be of some practical value. Waterworth (1983) is an example of using a taxonomy of 'dialogue acts' in interactive dialogue construction. The success of such an approach depends, of course, on how well the classes of 'dialogue act' identified account for the required range of interactive behaviours, and the extent to which these dialogue acts can be identified from short samples of such behaviour.

6.2.2. Indirect Speech Acts

Speech Act Theory is a theory of action, not of meaning. Utterances do not have underlying semantic representations that account for their effects. Rather, they have effects by virtue of the force that has come to be associated with them. Illocutionary force is thus explained in terms of pragmatics, because it depends on the felicity conditions being satisfied in the circumstances of an utterance being produced, rather than on the ordinary semantics of truth and falsity. Theories that rest on semantics fail to account for performatives, for example when utterances which are clearly false are felicitously made, since semantic theories suggest that performatives become true through being felicitously uttered. According to Levinson (1983) both approaches suggest that the force of an utterance is reflected in its literal form. Speech Act Theory claims that literal forms come to have illocutionary force associated with them by conventional usage. Both views have trouble accounting for Indirect Speech Acts (ISAs). ISAs are utterances such as "Could you pass the salt ?" or "I wonder if you would mind passing the salt ?" or "Can you reach the salt ?" or "Is there any salt down that end ?" They appear to achieve functions (like requesting that the addressee passes the salt to the speaker) indirectly, and the same function can be achieved in a great variety of indirect ways, perhaps too many ways for their effects to be reflected in their literal form.

The main problem with Speech Act theory, as Brown and Yule (1983) point out, is that it "does not offer the discourse analyst a way of determining how a particular set of linguistic elements, uttered in a particular conversational context, comes to receive a particular interpreted meaning". However, they also suggest that "the problem with identifying speech acts should not necessarily lead the analyst to abandon their investigation".

6.2.3. Other Speech Act Approaches

Levinson (1983) points out two ways in which it might be claimed that the idea of literal form reflecting force could be saved: idiom theory, and inference theory. Idiom theory suggests that the indirectness of ISAs is illusory. Such sentences are actually idiomatic forms of sentences with literal force. But, as Levinson notes, the list of idiomatic expressions then becomes almost infinitely long, there is no clear indication of which idiomatic interpretation should be applied in a particular case, and ISAs generally work across languages whereas idioms should be localised. According to inference theories, intended meaning is computed by participants in a conversation. The formation of such inferences is triggered in some way such that the participants know that literal force is inadequate, and inference rules exist for working out intended force from literal form and situational context. Levinson suggests a more radical alternative. Perhaps sentences do not have literal force at all, in which case there are no ISAs (or, to put it another way, all speech acts are indirect). Illocutionary force resides entirely in the realm of pragmatics (as opposed to depending on the interpretation of literal force through pragmatics, as Speech Act Theory suggests). One such pragmatic theory of speech acts is 'Context-Change Theory'.

According to Context-Change Theory, Speech Acts are seen as operations on contexts. A context here is a set of propositions about what is the case in a situation. An utterance changes the context by altering at least one of the set of propositions that comprises the context. For example, by asserting that P is the case, a speaker changes the context from one in which the speaker is not committed to P, to one in which he is. The theory can be rigorously expressed in set-theoretic terms, with no appeal to intentions. Levinson (1983), however, doubts the generality of such a theory. Does it really apply to the full range of acts economically? Can any Speech Act type theory really be viable given that they all attempt to fit utterances into a limited set of categories of one sort or another? He argues that this is either trivially easy (if literal form reflects force exactly), or context plays such a large role in the interpretation of the functions of utterances that the notion of Speech Acts adds little or nothing to the analysis. But within the constrained context of a particular application domain, such as human-computer interaction on a particular topic, this may not be such a damning criticism. Other approaches merit serious consideration, however.

6.2.4. The Demise of Speech Act Theories

Speech Act Theory emphasised the idea that utterances are used by their speakers to achieve functions, i.e. they are used to do things in situations, not merely to describe states of affairs. But Speech Act theories have problems if they adhere to the notion of literal force, particularly in the case of Indirect Speech Acts. They also tend to take inadequate account of the role of contextual information in the interpretation of the function of utterances in particular situations. It is claimed that they cannot cope with contextual factors adequately without becoming so complex as to lose their value. As the importance of context is more widely appreciated, Speech Act approaches are being undermined by work based on the empirical study of natural language use (see Chapter 7). The notion of the Speech Event, defined as a culturally recognised social activity in which an utterance has a specific, specialised role, is gaining credence. The suggestion is that to use language in contexts, speakers and hearers make use of inferencing within a cultural- and activity-specific framework of expectations about that activity, social roles, and so on. One way of looking at this is to say that people attempt to use an appropriate mental structure to interpret any speech event. One such structure is the frame (Minsky, 1975), which is discussed later in this chapter.

6.2.5. In Conclusion

Despite the limitations of Speech Act approaches outlined above, the idea of speech or dialogue acts, of utterances reflecting a limited set of underlying functions that speakers are attempting to achieve, may yet be useful in the realm of human-computer interaction, where the purposes of discourse are clearly, and as yet necessarily, more restricted than in human-human conversations. In other words, for our purposes, the notion of illocutionary force as discussed above, can be replaced by the concept of conversational function. But even in the case of such human-computer interaction, account must be taken of situation-specific knowledge about how 'speech events' are used to perform such dialogue acts. Such inferencing behaviour is necessary to identify speech events in particular contexts.

The way in which conversational behaviour is used to achieve underlying functions can only be identified by looking at actual conversations in particular settings. Ways of representing situation-specific knowledge are outlined in 6.3 (below). Ways of gathering the knowledge to be represented, which depend on the capture and analysis of conversational behaviour in appropriate contexts, are covered in Chapter 7.

This brief review of some current theoretical approaches to the interpretation of language in use has focussed on speech acts, and closely related, approaches. Some other ways of looking at language behaviour are mentioned in the next section, where we focus on issues of knowledge representation.

6.3.   COMPARISON   OF   ALTERNATIVE   REPRESENTATION SCHEMES

6.3.1. Introduction

Knowledge Representation (KR) is one of the key issues in Artificial Intelligence (AI). Knowledge is represented in computer systems by means of a combination of data structures and interpretive procedures. There are a handful of different ways in which this has been attempted, but there is no theory on which to base the selection of a KR technique for a particular task. It is not known, in any systematic way, why some schemes are good for certain tasks and not for others, nor, in some cases, whether or not a particular KR scheme is optimal for a particular application. There are two aspects to such KR for dialogue contruction; the representation of the dialogue itself, and the representation of relevant background knowledge.

In principle, exactly the same knowledge can be represented by means of a variety of general- and special-purpose KR schemes. Some systems (and perhaps humans) use a range of techniques to do the same thing in a variety of ways, or to do different aspects of the job (e.g. HEARSAY-II; see Erlman & Lesser, 1980). The schemes vary in the way the two KR aspects, data structures (facts) and interpretive procedures (heuristics, inferencing), are achieved. This affects the relative ease of use of these two components, which tend to be opposed; if the fact-base is easy to examine and change, the inferencing component tends not to be, and vice versa.

The following sections briefly review KR techniques and some of the criteria that have been used for their informal assessment.

6.3.2.   Criteria for Assessing Knowledge Representation Techniques

There are no formal metrics for judging the appropriateness of a particular KR scheme. Choices must be made in the light of the application, but there is no principled way of arriving at a decision in advance of the construction of actual implementations. However, certain criteria on which KR schemes may be compared can be identified. The following characteristics are suggested (modified from Barr & Feigenbaum, 1981).

6.3.2.1.   Scope and grain size

Scope is the breadth of KR in terms of the amount of the world at large that can, in principle, be represented. Grain size refers to the detail with which individual entities are represented, and the extent to which the detail can be utilised by the inferencing component. However, what cannot be easily judged a priori is the detail required for a particular application and, thus, the ease of use of a KR scheme of a particular grain size and scope.

6.3.2.2. Indeterminacy and semantic primitives

Indeterminacy refers to the fact that the same formalism could be used to represent facts in lots of different ways. The attributes of the application that are used as basic units (semantic primitives) are also a matter of choice. Again, a priori decisions are difficult; such questions are best answered in practice.

6.3.2.3. Modularity, understandability, and modifiability

It is claimed that modular schemes have advantages, because parts of the knowledge base can be readily changed without upsetting other parts. Modular systems are also supposed to be more easily understood by people, because the meaning of data structures is independent of the context of the system as a whole. But, a lot of human knowledge appears to be non-modular and cannot be readily expressed as independent rules or facts. Conversational behaviour may well be the sort of application where independence of this sort is difficult to achieve and, perhaps, inappropriate. Independence as applied to both the data structure and the reasoning component cannot be achieved. Typically, in modular systems the facts are independent and easy to recognise and change predictably, but the reasoning process is not. In relatively nonmodular systems (e.g. those that use a largely procedural KR scheme) the reasoning component is easily understood and modified, but the facts are scattered throughout the knowledge base and are hard to identify. Production Systems, and some Logics, are intrinsically modular; frames, procedural representations and networks are arguably not.

6.3.2.4. Declarative versus procedural

KR schemes fall somewhere on a continuum between the extremes of being fully declarative and being fully procedural. Typically, the greater the declarative element in a scheme the more modular the system can be; the facts are independent, understandable and readily modified, but the reasoning may not be. Enthusiasts also claim greater flexibility and economy, as well as completeness and certainty of deduction, for declarative representation schemes. Although the facts are less independent and harder to understand and change with procedural schemes, the reasoning component is easier to code and understand, and domain-specific heuristics can be used to focus on appropriate lines of reasoning. It is generally recognised that a mix of declarations and procedures is needed for most applications, the flavour of the mix depending on the particular application. Procedural schemes have proved useful for some natural language applications (e.g. Winograd, 1973). A promising approach, is the use of procedural attachment (e.g. Winograd, 1975; Bobrow et al., 1977).

6.3.2.5. Psychological validity

If the aim is to mirror in some way the way in which humans represent knowledge for cognitive processing, then the question of psychological validity becomes relevant. And as language is a product of the human mind, it is plausible that the structure of language, and of minds, are suited to each other, although the structure of mind is very poorly understood, of course. It seems at least possible that KR approaches that have some psychological validity, as far as language is concerned, are likely to have value for language-based applications. Psychological validity has been claimed for procedural representations (when dealing with language) and also for network systems (as models of memory, e.g. Quillian, 1968) although not all of the many varieties of nets and networks are intended as psychological models. Schank and his co-workers make strong claims about the psychological validity of script-based approaches (e.g. Schank, 1982; Schank & Abelson, 1977). Production Systems have also been suggested as a valid model of the mechanisms involved in the psychological phenomena of selective attention, limited capacity, and executive control (e.g. Allport, 1980), and even human cognition in general (Newell, 1980). The propositional approach of, for example, van Dijk (1977) has been claimed as the way humans store and interpret information contained in discourse. Kintsch (1974) suggests that the number of underlying propositions contained in a piece of written text predicts how long it will take to read and remember that text. The notion of 'opportunistic planning', using a flexible control strategy such as a 'blackboard', has been suggested as a model of human planning (Hayes-Roth, 1980). It seems quite likely that humans actually use multiple representation and problem solving methods, which can be brought to bear on different sorts of activity, different aspects of the same activity, or to redundantly tackle the same problem.

6.3.3. A Brief Review of Selected KR Techniques

The following points up a few of the available KR techniques, with brief comments on each. Some KR schemes can be seen as relatively neutral in terms of their relationship to theories of the way we produce and understand language. Others (e.g. scripts, propositions, planning) imply particular underlying theoretical assumptions. Indeed, some KR schemes could be legitimately described as language theories. It should be noted that what follows highlights the differences between underlying principles. In reality, most workers use a combination of methods, rather than concentrating on one to the exclusion of all others.

6.3.3.1. Logic

First-order predicate logic is a powerful language for problem solving, based on the fundamental notion of truth and falsity. Statements formulated in appropriate syntactic form can be operated upon by established inference rules to derive new statements. A description of the ways in which logic may be used for knowledge representation will not be attempted here.

Some people claim that logic is a natural way to represent and solve problems, but this seems to depend on the nature of the problem. Logic is certainly precise, with an unambiguous interpretation. It is very flexible - it can be applied to a wide range of problem types. Logical representations can be highly modular. They are monotonic, in the sense that new facts can be added to existing statements without affecting what follows from the earlier statements. Given that logic intrinsically deals with matters of truth and falsity, it could be argued that it is not the most appropriate formalism for representing linguistic dialogue behaviour, given the reservations, expressed by speech act theorists, about the validity of truth conditions as applied to such behaviour.

Although the representation of facts is clear in logic, that of the processing component is not (i.e. logic representations suffer from the problems of modular, declarative schemes referred to above). This problem led to the revival of interest in procedural representation schemes in the 1970s. There are, however, several logics available, and these may be incorporated in schemes using a variety of knowledge structures (such as plans and scripts).

6.3.3.2. Propositions

Closely related to logic is an approach that rests on the postulation of propositions that define the meaning of language samples (e.g. van Dijk, 1977). That is, it is suggested that the meaning of an utterance, or piece of written text, can be fully captured as a set of propositions. The claim is that speakers and hearers share a common underlying representation of meaning, from which the speaker produces an utterance, and into which the hearer decodes that utterance. The more propositions into which a sample of discourse can be 'decomposed' the longer it will take to read and remember (Kintsch, 1974). This view of language production and understanding is in opposition to some of the linguistic theories outlined earlier. It seems to suggest that contextual factors are of little or no relevance, that the meaning of an utterance is independent of the circumstances in which it is uttered. Context-Change Theory can be seen as a propositional approach that avoids this criticism. By this view, propositions represent the context of an utterance, the performance of a speech act modifying the situation by changing one or more propositions.

6.3.3.3. Production systems

Production Systems (PSs) consist of 3 parts; a rule-base full of sets of production rules, a data structure of facts, also known as the context or the short-term memory buffer, and an interpreter or inference engine. Production rules have a left-hand side or condition part, and a right-hand side or action part. The condition part consists of the "If such and such, and so and so" element; the action part is the "then do such and such" element which can fire when the condition part is satisfied. Conditions are satisfied when they are present in the data structure, actions are fired when they are carried out by the interpreter. The interpreter also has rules about when to fire actions when conditions are satisfied.

There is a wide variety of ways in which PSs can be implemented. They have the general advantages of being highly modular (at least for relatively small PSs) and of exhibiting uniformity of knowledge in the rule-base. This may make them (the production rules) easier to understand and modify. However, the flow of control is less obvious and understandable. The representation of 'what to do if such and such is true' type knowledge seems to naturally suggest a production rule approach, and is easily understood. But operation of the algorithms specifying the flow of control amongst productions is hidden and seems unnatural and hard to follow. Their modular and uniform structure also makes them inefficient; they cannot easily be made to chunk actions into useful larger sequences, for example.

PSs seem to be good for doing tasks that require the integration of a large number of separate facts or independent actions. They are less good for situations where facts cannot be easily separated from the way they are used (i.e. where representation and control are interdependent). PSs may thus be good for some language-related tasks, but not for others.

6.3.3.4. Procedural descriptions

Procedural descriptions state explicitly how to do things, as opposed to the declarative function of stating what is the case. The use of procedural knowledge has the advantages outlined in 3.2.4, above. Procedural description has often been applied in language-based interactive systems of varying complexity, and it could be argued that, as conversation is intrinsically procedural in some sense, procedural descriptions are a natural way of implementing conversational strategies.

The procedural approach makes the way in which the flow of control changes as a result of contributions from the enquirer (in an information providing system) very easy to follow. Procedural descriptions are likely to be useful in analysing conversational behaviour (see Chapter 7), and can thus feed directly into the implementation of corresponding strategies.

6.3.3.5. Nets and networks

Various approaches have been taken to using semantic networks, i.e. formalisms based on nodes (boxes, circles, or whatever) and arcs (lines joining nodes). Both are typically labelled, with the nodes representing things (objects, situations, actions, etc.) and the arcs indicating relations between the things. Approaches differ in the way inferences are drawn, in the actual meaning attached to the common formalism used. Unlike logic, different semantic network schemes do not share a formal semantics; the notation is used to mean different things by different workers.

Network approaches have proved very popular for large representation tasks. They are regarded as well suited to situations where reasoning is based on a complicated taxonomy, as in the work of Woods and his associates (e.g. Woods et al., 1972). They cater easily for the inheritance of properties, so that things like expectations and default assumptions can be readily represented. There is evidence that in some applications, and for some individuals, networks are easier to use than, for example, production systems (Guest, 1982).

A problem with networks is choosing a viable way of directing searches of the network structure, which otherwise becomes excessively inefficient and lengthy for anything but trivial tasks. Various ways of directing search have been tried, often involving imposing some structure on the underlying network. Another approach to the same problem was the work on frame-based representations, which can be regarded as being derived from earlier semantic network approaches.

Other problems with networks include deciding on how meaning should be represented, and the computational demands produced by large databases referred to above.

6.3.3.6. Frames, and frame-like schemes

Frames were devised by Minsky (1975) as a knowledge representation scheme that would enhance the capability of systems to deal with the sort of real world information people handle so effortlessly. Kuipers (1975) gives a good account of the underlying principles, and only the briefest of descriptions is attempted here.

Frames are an attempt at organising knowledge in a way that maps onto the real world problem that is being addressed. New information can be accommodated within this organisation, so that previous experience in a given context can guide what is expected. This is achieved by the structure of frames, each of which possess slots that define particular aspects of a thing, a concept, or a situation. Frames can be seen as buckets with handles. The handle names the frame so it can be referenced, and typically says something about the status of the frame; the bucket is full of holes, called 'slots', to be filled with handles of other frames, or actual values. Slots may have default values, and may be optional. When expectations are violated, a new structure (a new frame) may be generated. An important feature of frames is the way properties are inherited from frames representing a kind of thing in general, to specific, detailed cases. Another crucial feature is the way frame systems combine declarative descriptions of properties with procedures which are attached to particular slots. This notion of procedural attachment has been suggested as a way of avoiding the pitfalls of purely declarative or procedural approaches (Winograd, 1975). One of the hard things to grasp about frames is the fact that they are, in a sense, autonomous. Each frame has its own pieces of knowledge and its own goals. It inherits properties from parent frames, and in the course of achieving its goals it may change its own slot values, refer to other frames, or cause new frames to be generated. Potential problems lie in the areas of dialogue specification, program understandability, and modifiability (see Section 6.4, below).

Another popular approach that developed out of the frame concept, but which was aimed specifically at representing sequences of events in particular, rather stereotyped, situations is that of scripts (e.g. Schank & Abelson, 1977). The best known example is the restaurant script dealing with acceptable sequences of behaviour across a range of types of eating establishment. Other formalisms with strong similarities to the original frame conception include 'scenarios' (Sanford & Garrod, 1981) and 'schemata' (e.g. Anderson, 1977; Rumelhart, 1975).

6.3.3.7. Mental models

An alternative to the idea that understanding depends on breaking down sentences into underlying units of meaning (as with logic and propositions), and to the popular idea that it depends on the use of stereotypical structures (frames, scripts, etc.), was put forward by Johnson-Laird (e.g. 1981). A mental model can be seen as "a representation in the form of an internal model of the state of affairs characterised by the sentence" (Brown & Yule, 1983). Models are constructed, usually in order of likelihood in relation to past experience, and manipulated to test whether the models behave as would be predicted from what is going on in the text (or the situation). When failures occur, new, refined models are constructed and tested. This view can, in at least some cases, predict the difficulties people have with certain sentences (which do not lead to good initial models, for example), and with the sometimes illogical conclusions most people come to when presented with a set of related facts. This view implies that, in producing and understanding language, people do not use inferences to arrive at meaning, contrary to some of the linguistic approaches outlined earlier. The main problem with this approach is implementing it; the practical details of how we create, select, and use such mental constructions are obscure, despite their intuitive appeal.

6.3.3.8. Plans

Planning is more legitimately categorised as a goal-directed problem solving technique, rather than a knowledge representation scheme, but plan-based approaches do carry with them assumptions about the representation of knowledge and, indeed, about the nature of language-based interaction. Planning approaches to language can be seen as a reaction against linguistic orientations that neglect the purposes for which utterances are made, the functions they achieve by their performance (see, for example, Power, 1978). This can be viewed as a practical consequence of the speech act approaches to linguistics which, as we saw earlier, stress the use to which language is put in practice, not merely the way it can be used to represent facts. There are several different ways in which planning has been implemented, such as nonhierarchical planning, hierarchical planning, the use of stored plans (similar to Schank's work with Scripts), and 'opportunistic' planning (intended to model human planning strategies).

The link between planning and speech act theory is explicit in the work of Allen (e.g. Allen, 1983), which suggests that understanding a speaker's intention from a question can be achieved, in some cases at least, by the use of plan-based knowledge and of structures that represent actions. Allen (1983) demonstrates how a planning approach can be used to identify intentions. This involves plan construction and inferencing (where plan inferencing refers to the reconstruction of another's plan on the basis of that person's observed behaviour).

6.4. DIALOGUE SPECIFICATION FOR LANGUAGE-BASED INTERACTION

This section briefly reviews some issues relating to the ways in which dialogue control for language-based systems can be achieved. Initially, the idea of discrete dialogue control modules, and the way these affect dialogue design practice, is introduced. A few alternative ways of dialogue specification and the criteria for their assessment are then discussed. Finally, the use of 'frame' systems in this context is considered in more detail.

6.4.1. Discrete Dialogue Controllers

It is generally accepted, within the human-computer interaction community, that significant advantages accrue from separating the user interface portion of systems from the background application software, and having convenient and appropriate ways of specifying the former (e.g. Edmonds, 1978, 1981, 1982; Hayes, 1984; Hayes et al., 1985; Schulert et al., 1985; Tanner & Buxton, 1983), i.e. from the creation of discrete 'Dialogue Controllers' (DCs) using suitable 'Dialogue Control Languages' (DCLs).

There appears to be little consistency in the way these concepts are named; DCs are also known as 'Dialogue Managers', and 'Interface (or Interaction) Handlers', while DCLs have been referred to as 'Dialogue Specification (or Development) Languages (or Systems)', 'User Interface Management Systems (or Languages)', 'Dialogue Generators' and, confusingly, 'Dialogue Managers'. In the present document DC refers to the part of the system that determines what happens at the user interface, and DCL to the language in which that part of the system is implemented.

It should be noted that 'dialogue' here refers to everything that passes between the user and the system in either direction, using quasi-natural language as the medium of exchange.

6.4.1.1. Dialogue design

DCLs are used to specify and control the dialogue between the system and its users. They can also be seen as the interface between the interface designer and the user interface. As Edmonds (1982) points out, it is not enough for the interface designer (who may, or may not, be the applications programmer as well) to be aware of the principles of good human-computer dialogue design, he must also have a suitable interface through which to express such design principles, i.e. a DCL that is also a good Dialogue Design Language (DDL). A good DDL would have built into it the sorts of function that facilitate good dialogue design. There will frequently be conflicts between the needs of dialogue specification and control, and dialogue design; this means that one language is unlikely to satisfy the requirements of both a good DCL and a good DDL. One solution is for the dialogue designer to interact with the DCL via a DDL written specifically for the purpose of dialogue design. Note, however, that there is a danger of infinite regress here. Providing a good interface for the interface designer requires someone to design that interface (the interface to the interface), who in turn requires a good interface to the interface to the interface, and so on.

Without going this far, the notion of a DDL buffer is gaining credibility. The DDL is provided as a means whereby the "dialogue author" can interact with the DCL. Hartson and Johnson (1983) see the dialogue author as "a skilled communication specialist whose ultimate goal is to create and implement human-factored dialogues", and who is concerned with "the high level sequencing of computer-user interaction, as well as the form, style and content of specific dialogues". He is not a programmer, however, and uses special tools (such as a DDL 'buffer') to create a dialogue design that can be embodied in the DCL as the DC itself. Johnson, Hartson, and others expand on the role of dialogue author in a recent volume (Ehrlich & Williges, 1986). Many workers have attempted to combine the roles of DCL (the language in which the DC is actually implemented) and DDL (the language used to design possible dialogues). It is perhaps to be expected that such an approach will inevitably result in a trade-off between ease of dialogue design (the DDL emphasis) and sophistication of dialogue control (the DCL emphasis).

6.4.1.2. Advantages of DCs

Even if the extra discrete level of a DDL is not attempted, the construction of a discrete (conceptually if not physically) DC to handle the human computer interface, with a DCL that is reasonably convenient (from a dialogue design point of view) for expressing the nature of that interface is generally recognised to be a desirable state of affairs. Hayes et al. (1985) suggest the following principal advantages of this approach:

(1) Because DCs typically employ abstractions of interface behaviour, definitions of interfaces are concise and directly programmable.

(2)   The ease of user interface specification afforded by DCLs means that effort saved can be directed towards the construction of more intelligent and supportive interfaces, offering good error correction facilities, automatic help, etc.

(3)   Human Factors specialists can more readily contribute to the interface design. The jobs of application programming and dialogue specification are separated. The latter can be left to Human Factors people, who can modify and experiment with the interface independently from the applications programming.

(4)   Interfaces, and their specification, can be made more consistent.

(5)   Conversely, different interface specifications can be developed for the same application. This permits comparisons of different possible interface designs, use of interfaces with different I/O devices, and catering for varying user skill levels and preferences.

Other advantages include the possibilities for rapid prototyping and iterative development (Schulert et al., 1985).

6.4.1.3. Conclusion

There is potential value in thinking of the user interface as controlled by a separate and distinct (virtual) machine - the DC; and we should express the characteristics of the DC in a DCL that is convenient for the interface designer (or, better still, implement a dialogue design module in a DDL designed for this purpose). Interface design should be given due importance; it is central to the production of a usable system. It should not be seen as a relatively minor aspect of system construction to be sorted out once the application software has been written. Indeed, there is justification for arguing that the user interface should be designed first, then the system can be developed around this design. The design of the user interface, and of the underlying application, require completely different skills and expertise (Schulert et al., 1985); it is therefore often preferable for them to be carried out by different people.

The separation of information flows between the system and user (the dialogue), from underlying task execution (the application) has certain advantages, but does not, in itself, solve the problems of designing a good dialogue. Rather, it makes dialogue decisions easier to implement and test. The decisions to be made cover the style of the interaction and the actual content of the dialogue, in terms of information conveyed and interpreted, and the allocation and flow of control between system and user. It has been suggested that there are actually no scientific a priori guidelines for making such decisions because, amongst other things, cognitive theories in this area are immature, experimental data is sparse and may be ungeneralisable or conflicting (Cockton, 1985). By this view, all dialogue decisions must be made according to field observations of user behaviour and the application processing must be insulated from the inevitable changes to the information flow structure (dialogue) such observations will necessitate. Separation of dialogue and background processing facilitates this insulation.

6.4.2. Approaches

6.4.2.1. Some alternatives

It is known that certain methods of dialogue specification are easier to use than others, though this varies with the expertise of the designers. For example, specification in sets of production rules is often contrasted with the use of recursive transition networks (e.g. Alty, 1983; Edmonds, 1982). Guest (1982) reports a comparison of the two approaches. He found that the network approach was generally the more successful.

Several dialogue control systems and languages have appeared in recent years, as the need for good dialogue design has become more generally recognised. Most of these have as their rationale the notion of a discrete DC written in a DCL that allows (i) rapid prototyping, (ii) transparency to the dialogue designer, (iii) readily modifiable dialogue structure (without detailed knowledge of the applications software - i.e. built-in 'human factorability'). Two important dimensions along which they may be categorised are the mode of interaction, and the support given to the dialogue designer.

Many DCs were originally conceived for use with screen-based, or multi-modal interactive systems (e.g. Hayes et al., 1985; Tanner & Buxton, 1983) This tends to result in a certain bias in their mode of operation, towards menu selection, for example. Dealing with language obviously raises particular problems, although some DCs for language-based interaction have adhered to the notion of a discrete component aimed at aiding the dialogue designer (e.g. Leicester Polytechnic's SYNICS system.

It has been suggested that there are no proven models for what makes a good DC, but that the DCL may be chosen without reference to the specific type of DC (e.g. Cockton, 1985). Several models for DC structure have, of course, been suggested, such as networks (e.g. SYNICS, RAPID/USE), production systems, logic, and frames (e.g. GUS, UFL), amongst others. Some lend themselves more readily to the notions of discrete and 'human-factorable' DC creation than others, and frames and logic appear less amenable to this approach than some of the other specification formalisms at first sight, but there is no theory of human-computer interaction on which to base the choice of model. These approaches can only be compared after implementation, but most current implementations are not entirely faithful to the model on which they are based, so the models cannot really be compared by this means.

In terms of the degree of support given to the dialogue designer, available systems fall into three main categories. Some employ a DCL that is intended to be easy and convenient for the dialogue designer to interact with directly, and which insulates him from the complexities of the underlying software (e.g. SYNICS, RAPID/USE). Others use a DDL for dialogue construction, but a different part of the system runs the dialogue, which may or may not be by means of a discrete DC (e.g. ISPF Program Development Facility; see IBM, 1983). Finally there are those, such as GUS, which employ a discrete DC but do not attempt to cater for the particular needs of the dialogue designer. Network-based systems seem particularly well suited to the needs of the dialogue designer, but lack some of the power of frames and logic programming.

6.4.2.2. Criteria for assessment

Whatever the means of its construction, a good human-computer dialogue, as Stewart (1980) points out, "is a complex series of interacting components..." that "...must be tested out early with real users and be developed in conjunction with them". It was widespread recognition of the need for early testing with system-naive subjects that led to the development of DCs and their DCLs (and, later, to DDLs). Good DCLs are thus those which permit the rapid construction of human-computer dialogues in a form that is understandable, and thus readily modifiable in the light of exposure to users other than the programmers of the system. They must also, of course, have the capabilities to carry out the interactive tasks required of them. We can thus identify four main criteria with which to assess DCLs, as follows:

(1)   Power - a DCL should have the functions and flexibility to carry out the target interactive operations.

(2)   Ease of Dialogue Specification - it should be possible to use the DCL to produce a prototype DC, implementing a particular, chosen, style of interaction, quickly and easily, without necessarily understanding the system as a whole.

(3)   Transparency - the DC should be expressible in the DCL in such a way that its operation is not hidden amongst a mass of other functions.

(4)   Modifiability - following from (2) and (3), above, it should be
      possible to quickly and easily change the dialogue, in under-
      standable ways, following exposure of the DC to system-naive
      trialists.

6.4.3. Frames

Frame languages are a way of representing knowledge based on the
concept of 'frames' (Minsky, 1975), see 6.3 (above). A fairly well
known example is KRL - Knowledge Representation Language
(Bobrow & Winograd, 1977). Such languages have been used to produce interactive database query systems for some years, as for example the 'Genial Understanding System' or GUS (Bobrow et al., 1977)
offering flight information and booking service.

A frame language can be categorised as a DCL, and the frame program written in that language to control the interactive dialogue
comprises the DC.

6.4.3.1. Frames for dialogue control

Any DC dealing with relatively unpredictable user responses
and/or sequencing of responses will be reasonably complex in its
functioning, because of the number of possible routes the dialogue
may take, but this does not mean the DCL need be complex from the
dialogue designer's point of view - indeed, the more transparent the
better in this respect. A good DC would thus be capable of handling
the intrinsic complexity of flexible dialogue structuring, while at the
same time facilitating easy dialogue specification and modification by
the interface designer.

Frame systems typically embody various interactive strategies in the
form of small programs designed to be highly separable and thus,
potentially at least, modifiable. But these programs are often difficult
to write and understand. What seems to be lacking is a buffer between
the dialogue designer and the DC. The DCL would ideally present a
face to the dialogue designer to facilitate dialogue specification and
modification, while protecting the designer from the underlying complexity of the DC.

Frames can be used to produce very flexible dialogue structures that
seem more natural, because of the potential for variability, than more
deterministic approaches. This is the other side of the DC complexity
coin. It may not be possible in practice for relatively non-
deterministic DC systems to achieve the degree of transparency
required for easy dialogue design without the creation of a further
level of abstraction - a Dialogue Design Language (DDL) - that can

be distinguished from the DCL itself. But this clearly introduces another designer into the process, and the construction of the DDL would itself be a large task. But certain facilitating features could be incorporated into the DC fairly readily, such as the ability to change output messages easily.

Frame languages, when used for language-based dialogue specification, are principally aimed at fulfilling the requirements of a DCL which, as mentioned earlier, will sometimes be in conflict with those of a good DDL, or at least will have different priorities. As with GUS, and indeed following directly from the 'knowledge in frames' approach, they incorporate procedures that might more normally be regarded as background tasks in DC systems. It is perhaps inevitable that non-deterministic systems cannot retain a functionally distinct unit that is only concerned with the dialogue between system and user (the usual, discrete DC).

For dialogue control to be completely separable, it must be predictable. It is not clear that a non-deterministic knowledge-based approach is most suited to language-based dialogues within strictly confined domains, especially those using speech (where the need to recognise inputs places severe restrictions on likely inputs to the DC). A deterministic approach to a system of similar complexity is the Bell Labs airline information and reservation system (Levinson & Shipley, 1979). For developing systems that operate with speech within restricted information domains, a deterministic DC will allow the design and further modification of usable human-computer dialogues in a disciplined way.

Frame languages are clearly a powerful means of representing knowledge, with capabilities well suited to carrying out sophisticated, knowledge-based dialogue control in the realm of quasi-natural language. But frames appear less convenient for the design of the dialogue itself. This partly reflects the nature of non-deterministic systems, but is also due to the fact that frames are not primarily aimed at providing a tool for dialogue design but, rather, at implementing the functions of the DC. Problems exist in the areas of (1) ease of dialogue specification, (2) transparency, and (3) modifiability.

(1)   Initial dialogue specification is not particularly easy, although this is not to say that the functions the dialogue designer would want to have implemented cannot be carried out. It is just rather difficult to adopt certain approaches.

(2)   Frame programs are not easy to follow. The way the dialogue operates is far from transparent, thus problem areas can be difficult to spot quickly.

(3)   Changing dialogues in a predictable way is not straightforward, i.e. frame programs are not readily modifiable. This means that

dialogue strategies cannot be prototyped rapidly; and fast, iterative test and development is not a realistic possibility.

Frames can provide a good DCL for language-based interaction in some ways, but are not, as yet, a convenient tool for dialogue design. To achieve this frame languages need to provide facilities such that programs are more readily specifiable, transparent and, thus, modifiable. An alternative would be to develop an intervening Dialogue Development Language environment to mediate between the aims of the dialogue designer and the complexities of the frame language.

6.5. CONCLUSION

To be successful, language-based interface design depends on considerations from linguistics and knowledge representation being combined with appropriate dialogue specification techniques and tools. To move towards speech-based interaction in a conversational manner, human interactive speech strategies must also be analysed and incorporated into the dialogue design process. The next chapter focusses on these conversational aspects, as well as on some current techniques and applications of current natural language processing.

7

Towards Conversational Systems

J. A. Waterworth

7.1. INTRODUCTION

Research on human-computer interaction via 'natural' language has, so far, tended to be decoupled from work on the design of speech interfaces. This chapter discusses the various strands that must be brought together to develop truly conversational systems successfully. An idealised conversational system would be capable of interacting in a natural and efficient way, as appropriate to a particular domain of discourse, speaking and listening to its interactant to achieve goals in a mixed-initiative manner. To achieve this end result, the system must obviously be capable of coping with the language the user will naturally use within the task domain. It must also know about conversational conventions for coping with the flow of control in an interactive speech dialogue. In this chapter work in both these areas is described.

A broad range of methods have been applied to the problems of providing human-computer interfaces that support some degree of interaction via 'natural language' (although no existing systems, even in research environments, allow interaction in totally unconstrained natural language). There have been two main strands to research in the area: (1) the provision of dialogue facilities for human-computer interaction, usually for particular applications or types of application, but also more theoretical issues of dialogue specification and representation; (2) 'natural language' approaches generally aimed more directly at developing techniques for understanding and generating an increasingly large subset of natural language. The theoretical issues involved in the two areas merge as, ultimately, true understanding and generation of language depends on taking knowledge about dialogue (and discourse generally, including conversation) into account.

Most 'pure' natural language research has focussed primarily on developing an understanding of the structure of language and expressing that structure in terms of computer programs, the test of these programs being how well they could generate or analyse written English (e.g. Mellish, 1985). This emphasis on form in NL contrasts with a growing concern with the uses of language within particular contexts. The basic premiss here is that in order to understand communication fully, any analysis of dialogue must incorporate some understanding of the aims speakers wish to achieve when they use language, i.e. what do speakers *do* with language? Some of the background to this area of research was covered in Chapter 6.

The next sections of this chapter cover some relatively unsophisticated methods for interpreting natural language, followed by a brief review of several current applications of this work. Dialogue aspects are the focus of later parts of the chapter, where the need to model human conversational strategies is proposed, and a research project aimed at identifying such strategies within particular domains is described.

7.2. NATURAL LANGUAGE PROCESSING (NLP)

7.2.1. Basic NLP Parsing Methods

A natural language understanding system will be characterised by some of three main components. At the simplest level, individual words or parts of words are identified and matched with entries in a lexicon. Morphological analysis, combined with an exceptions dictionary, is the usual approach. At the next level, some syntactic analysis on the basis of sentential structure is usually carried out, based on bottom-up or top-down parsing via rules or the construction of some form of transition network. The top level corresponds to arriving at some representation of the meaning of the sentence, the goal of understanding, from which some action can be performed, which may include the generation of suitable response in natural language (via the other two levels). How the semantics are derived from input strings from the user depends very much on the aims and application of the research.

7.2.1.1. 'Slot-and-frame'

'Slot-and-frame' approaches are based on a complete catalogue of all permissible inputs by the user. Essentially, all 'legal' sentences are described as frames, which contain slots that the user fills with particular tokens that allow the system to identify all of the input string. If the number of alternatives that the user may use at any one time is small, and if the user can be constrained in some way to use only those alternatives in a predictable way that conforms to a set of frames known to the system, then the approach is successful and efficient. Typically, the system must retain control and inform the user of the strictly limited range of options available at each point in the interaction. A typical application is data-base access on a restricted range of topics, with very limited semantic complexity. As the need to offer users the facility to specify a greater number of things in a wider variety of ways increases, this approach rapidly becomes impracticable.

7.2.1.2. Semantic parsing

One way of allowing users greater freedom in the construction of input strings is via 'semantic grammars'. Semantic grammars skip the stage of syntactic analysis and attempt to understand sentences in only two stages: lexical access, and semantic parsing. A semantic grammar is a set of rewrite rules that are used to convert sentences into a representation that the system can act on in some way. In general, the set of strings that can be interpreted corresponds quite closely to the underlying set of actions of the target program. They provide more flexibility than slot-and-frame approaches, but are still quite limited in applicability - only a relatively small subset of the language can be recognised. As the range of possibilities increases the rewrite rules, essentially created as hoc for each application, become too numerous to be specified practically.

Example of a simple rule set for semantic parsing

The following rule set defines what requests for information about train times can be recognised by a fictional database access interface. Lexical items (words) or combinations (phrases and sentences) not defined in the rule set cannot be interpreted. The rules thus cater for such utterances as 'I want to go to London on Saturday', 'I would like trains to Norwich on a weekday', or even 'Harwich Tuesday', but not 'Can you tell me the time of the next London train' or 'I would like details of trains to Norwich'. The set here is so small that it amounts to little more than a slot-and-frame grammar.

Train Request=BC/BFC/EBFC/GEBFC (where '/' means 'or')

B=B1/B2/B3/B4

C=C1/C2/D

B1='NORWICH'

B2='HARWICH'

B3='LOWESTOFT'

B4='LONDON'

C1='SATURDAY'

C2='SUNDAY'
D='WEEKDAY'/'MONDAY'/'TUESDAY'/'WEDNESDAY'/
'THURSDAY'/'FRIDAY'

E='TO'/'GO TO'/'TRAVEL TO'/'MY DESTINATION IS'

F='ON A'/'ON'/'TRAVEL ON'

G='I WOULD LIKE TRAINS'/'I WANT TO'/'I WANT DETAILS
OF'

7.2.1.3. Syntactic parsers

Syntactic grammars attempt to cater for the whole, or most, of a complete language. Such an approach is necessary to take advantage of the regularity inherent in all natural languages. Such grammatical regularity is independent of context detail, so an approach that allows parts of speech to be defined once only would appear very efficient. Unfortunately, syntactic parsing is not simple because of the complexity and ambiguity of natural language, with the same words, or even types of words, being used in a variety of ways (including ungrammatical constructions). In fact, no adequate syntactic parser for the whole of English has ever been written, and supposedly general-purpose parsers have, in the main, not been successful in particular applications. This has partly been due to the fact that the application program is not as sophisticated as the language-handling capabilities of the front-end, thus the system as a whole breaks down as users attempt to carry out impossible actions or make impossible requests for information. However, if the aim is to cater for a large subset of a natural language, then the syntactic regularities of the language must be capitalised upon via some method of syntactic parsing.

Linguists have looked in detail at ways of specifying the possibilities of a language in a body of rules, or some such formalism, for many years. Essentially, this has amounted to formulating techniques for syntactic parsing of varying degrees of adequacy. The techniques that have been used include augmented transition networks and chart parsing from phrase-structure rules, but it is not intended to provide a review of syntactic parsing techniques here.

There are also approaches such as case grammars which attempt to provide a link between syntactic and semantic parsing, but most attempts to bring the two approaches together have so far resulted in a fairly uncomfortable marriage.

7.2.1.4. Pragmatics

As discussed in Chapter 6, contextual knowledge of the world at large is often needed to make full sense of a particular piece of spoken or written language. This involves both knowledge of linguistic conventions about how people tend to do things with language in situations, and general knowledge about the world. Planning is one approach to handling the pragmatic use of language. Another is the attempt to arrive at a representation of the underlying conceptual structure, such as Schank's Conceptual Dependency Theory, which seeks to represent all actions in terms of a small number of semantic primitives.

7.2.2. NLP Applications 1: Text Understanding and Generation

Text understanding involves parsing inputs in some way suitable to the formation of a representation of text structure. Although written text has been the vehicle for much of this work, it could equally well (though with a few necessary enhancements!) be applied to recognised spoken language. The AI approach to understanding, and generating, meaningful text is to construct representations that can form the basis for generating replies to queries, producing summaries of content, etc.. If what is achieved matches what a human reader could manage, then the representations produced are held to be adequate as models of human behaviour. The quality of a text representation has been assessed by how good a summary it can be used to produce. As Alterman (1986) points out, these representations typically characterise perhaps one aspect of a text, but do not constitute complete understanding in the human sense. Thus the underlying representation of text is inadequate to support sophisticated summarisation. Two lines of research can be pursued to improve this situation. Firstly, alternative ways of representing more of the underlying text, so that fuller summaries can be produced, can be investigated. This raises issues of general knowledge of the world and how this can be represented, and, indeed, of representation formalisms, and how they relate to linguistic behaviour, as addressed earlier (Chapter 6). This is a very large task indeed. Another approach, advocated by Alterman (1986), is what he refers to as 'summarisation in the small', which does not involve attempting a representation that can model full human understanding. Rather, different smallscale representations of particular aspects of a body of text can form the basis of different forms of (in-the-small) summaries. The summaries can be seen as both the products, and the tests of, each underlying representation strategy. Essentially, then, the claim is that useful summaries, for particular purposes, can be produced on the basis of text representations of very limited sophistication. This makes summarisation a tractable problem for fairly short-term research, and relatively crude summarisers are already in use in real applications (see below).

7.2.2.1. Scanning

Scanning is a very limited form of language understanding, which could be regarded as an example of forming a representation suitable for summarisation-in-the-small. It has been applied to limited summarisation tasks, usually on short, telegraphic messages where the topics to be discussed are known in advance and the range of possibilities on each topic is strictly limited (Johnson, 1985). Pragmatic aspects of the message are predefined, thus simplifying the understanding task enormously. Syntax may be idiosyncratic or absent, but an approach based on the application of semantic parsing, or even slot-and-frame grammars, may be adequate.

7.2.2.2. Summarisation

FRUMP (Fast Reading Understanding and Memory Program) is an early example of automatic text understanding (Schank & Abelson, 1977). It 'skims', rather than understanding, and is a cut-down version of SAM. 'Sketchy scripts' are used, having only a few Conceptual Dependency (CD) representations, and causal connections are not usually included. It skims newspaper stories, already knowing what facts to look for. It does this on the basis of a list of expected facts (known as 'requests') specific to a particular type of story. When it has collected all the relevant requests its sketchy script is complete. Requests are in CD form with unfilled slots. FRUMP uses few requests per story type and produces a very brief summary. For example, its 'vehicle accident script' comprises 4 requests; (i) vehicle type, object hit, location, (ii) number of people killed, (iii) number of people injured, (iv) whose fault it was. FRUMP identifies which script is appropriate by looking in the first paragraph. It uses a semantic parser to convert phrases into CD representations, then matches these representations against requests in the script. Each script is stored (whether or not its requests are fully satisfied or not), so that new stories can be compared with old. If a match is found the new story is used to update the old, and the old is used to help interpret information in the new. It demonstrates its 'understanding' by constructing a simple summary from a sketchy script, e.g. "A train hit a train in Mexico. 17 people died. 45 people were injured". FRUMP demontrates what can be done using relatively simple techniques, which could be applied to recognised human speech as well as to written text. An obvious way of enhancing the system would be to improve the summary output component.

At the other end of the spectrum, Fum et al. (1985) describe their attempts at something more akin to human language understanding. They identify 3 stages in true summarisation:

(1)   Understanding the literal meaning of every sentence, including reference, quantification, and time.

(2)   Inferring and making explicit the macro-structure that accounts for global meaning and organisation, including coherence, rhetoric, and style.

(3)   Evaluating the relative importance of different conceptual units constituting the text.

Their work demonstrates the difficulty of achieving human-like understanding abilities. None of the stages above can, as yet, be fully realised.

7.2.3. NLP Applications 2: Quasi-Natural Language Interfaces

Interfaces that handle a small set of 'naturalish' language have been appearing gradually over the last few years, in areas where relatively simple techniques can yield dividends. These are distinguished from those above by the more interactive nature of their use. They can be seen as early steps towards conversational interfaces, although the techniques used have been no more sophisticated than those applied to the application areas above. Nor has much been done to make such interfaces truly natural, in the sense of similarity to human-human linguistic behaviour.

7.2.3.1. Database query

This area has received a great deal of attention in recent years. The use of electronic databases has increased greatly, and this growth seems likely to accelerate. Access to on-line sources of information is increasingly being offered by the purveyors of personal computers and office systems. Database access seems an obvious application for natural language interaction, since the domain of discourse appears restricted, and the alternatives, such as formal query languages, are so hard to use. Problems arise, however, from the fact that the user does not necessarily know what the domain handled by the system is, and will certainly have a different view of this domain, in details, than that embodied in the database. The language he would naturally use does not match the small set of words or phrases the system can accept, (as every on-line adventure game player will know).

So far, 'English-like' interfaces have been heavily promoted in the marketplace, with such fatuous descriptions as "Understands you just like your mom", although their capabilities are very restricted, and usually based on simple slot-and-frame type approaches. Work is in progress to develop more sophisticated 'query understanding' schemes, but it is not yet clear how successful these will be for a range of database applications. There seems to have been very little assessment of the success of such interfaces.

7.2.3.2. Text editing

An increasingly popular area for the provision of natural language interfacing is in the design of systems aimed at assisting the production and editing of documents in a word processing environment. In general, this involves attempting to suggest improvements to spelling, grammar, and style, as well as the usual facilities for copying, moving, filing, etc. Not surprisingly, since they are meant to be topic independent, the NLP element is predominantly syntactic. There is a discernible research trend towards incorporating some semantic elements, to support automatic filing and the production of preformed documents such as large-circulation letters, but this is not yet available in the marketplace. Advanced research projects are in progress to develop voice-controlled systems of this type, such as the 'voice-controlled word-processor', but it is not yet known whether this is a feasible application. Certainly, speech recognition will need to be better than is currently available, perhaps based on 'phonetic recognition' (see Chapter 2).

Such systems as "Writer's Workbench" (Bell Labs), and "Expert Editor" (Smart AI) go beyond checking words against a lexicon to provide style checking. The former (according to Johnson, 1985) assesses style by means of statistical techniques combined with simple linguistic processing. The latter is more sophisticated, being based on an expert system of 1500 rules, plus a lexicon of 50,000 technical words, to spot grammatical errors and ambiguities. "Epistle", a research project at IBM, goes further than "Writer's Worbench" in that it actually uses syntactic parsing techniques (augmented phrase strucure grammar), to enable more sophisticated word and style checking, as well as grammatical critiques.

7.2.3.3. NLP for speech applications

The combination of NLP techniques with speech I/O technology is, potentially, a powerful one, and developments along these lines are taking place in several areas, such as database access (e.g. the VODIS project, see below), and command interfaces (voice control of parts of systems).

Particular problems arise from the use of speech recognition, because of the limitations of the technology. Knowledge from higher sources (semantics, pragmatics, models of discourse) are being brought to bear to enhance recognition capabilities. This work falls under the 'dialogue construction' heading. But relatively simple appoaches can also enhance the effectiveness of an interface incorporating speech recognition. Simple slot-and-frame or semantic parsing can be used to support fairly sophisticated interfaces, such as the "Conversational Desktop" and "Put That There" interfaces developed at MIT Media Lab. (e.g. Schmandt, 1985).

On the synthesis side, text-to-speech conversion can be improved in quality if the synthesiser has some idea of the syntactic, and perhaps semantic, structure of the material to be delivered. As well as resolving pronunciation ambiguities this permits more intelligent selection of intonation forms, and of stress placement. This topic was covered in some detail in Chapter 2.

7.3. CONVERSATIONAL INTERFACES

7.3.1. Conversational Analysis and Dialogue Construction

This section is concerned with dialogue issues at the conversational level, where 'conversational' refers to the exchange of information, in a mixed-initiative manner, via alternating contributions from participants.

Two main theoretical approaches to the analysis of conversational data can be identified (Levinson, 1983): Discourse Analysis, and Conversational Analysis. Discourse Analysis attempts to extent the techniques of linguistics to units larger than the sentence, i.e. to establish a 'linguistics of dialogue'. The approach starts with theoretical assumptions about the way dialogue elements can be identified. It goes on to isolate these 'basic' elements and formulate rules for their combination into acceptable utterances. What is acceptable tends to depend on the intuitions of the analyst. This is an interesting and potentially useful approach, but with serious weaknesses. The main problem is that the data on which the theory is based, and exercised, tend to be very scant. Some would claim that the approach is overly and prematurely theoretical in nature, such that what is actually present in a broad range of conversational settings is overlooked. As a goal, though, a linguistics of dialogue is very appealing. Once the basic dialogue elements and the rules of combination were identified, dialogues could be implemented readily and with a large degree of automation. Some work has been done on the use of formal grammars for dialogue representation.

In contrast, Conversational Analysis can be criticised on the grounds that it is excessively atheoretical. Conversational Analysts insist on the collection of empirical data, unclouded by theoretical assumptions about basic elements or likely concatenation rules. As Levinson (1983) points out, "the methods are essentially inductive; search is made for recurring patterns across many records of naturally-occurring conversations, in contrast to the immediate categorisation of (usually) restricted data which is the typical first step in Discourse Analysis work". A useful way to tackle these issues for the future would be to adopt the Conversational Analysis approach initially, but retain the longer-term aim of arriving at the sorts of knowledge that could be formalised as the principles of a linguistics of dialogue (within particular contexts, if not generally). Conversational Analysis has already produced useful findings capable of implementation within conversing interactive systems (notably the work of the 'ethnomethodological' school, e.g. the concept of 'adjacency pairs' in Schegloff and Sacks (1973)). There are signs of a renewed surge of interest in this area, which has been relatively quiet since its heyday in the 1960s. A recent article on page 3 of the International Herald Tribune (Nov. 24, 1986) suggests that, under the new discipline of formal Conversational Analysis "even expression such as 'uh' or 'well' are viewed not as mistakes but as intentional expression of the rules of conversation".

A main focus of attention in applying this approach to interface design is the collection and analysis of conversational data, leading on to the implementation of dialogue models that embody the information gained from such analysis. Collection of data involves recording live conversations between participants, in a range of question and answering situations appropriate to target applications. One such exercise is described later in this chapter.

7.3.2. Identifying Interactive Strategies for Conversational Systems

The first part of this section outlines an approach to dialogue design for vocal, interactive information systems based on an analysis of human-human conversations in contexts similar to the target application. This is provided as a case study of the sort of work involved in collecting the some of the information needed to model human conversational strategies.

Three behavioural studies are briefly described. These led to the identification of conversational confirmation and correction strategies. It has already been suggested that behavioural studies of this type are essential, as the realisation of conversational strategies varies with discourse topic, Conversational Analysis provides a methodology for identifying the way conversational functions are achieved in practice.

In the second part, an experimental study investigating the effects of various methods of confirmation and correction is reported. This experiment compared transaction times for the vocal specification of varying number of items of information, with visual versus auditory feedback, and with global versus piecemeal spoken data entry. Since it is not yet possible to fully duplicate human performance because of, amongst other things, technological limitations on the capabilities of speech synthesisers and recognisers (especially the latter), this type of controlled experimental study is a necessary complement to the observation of naturally-occurring interactive behaviour.

7.3.2.1. Conversational analysis and VODIS dialogue design

The Voice Operated Database Inquiry System (VODIS) project aims to provide a natural-seeming, conversational interface, via advanced speech input and output techniques, to enable untrained members of the public to interact with databases by telephone, and without previous training or written instructions.

The dialogue design work for VODIS was founded on the idea that the study of human-human conversational behaviour, in a variety of conditions and under various constraints, can provide essential data to inform the process of designing human-computer dialogues for speech-based interaction. Vocal interrogation of database enquiry systems, combined with synthetic speech output from such systems, raises a host of questions about the way a system should prompt the user and what responses are to be expected at all stages of the interaction. Particularly problematic are such features as the best way to carry out confirmations and error recovery (essential with current speech recognition technology) and the prediction of the way users tend to volunteer information under a variety of conditions. Our previous work provided a starting point for research (Richards & Underwood, 1984; Underwood & Richards, 1984), but for VODIS it was decided that this approach should be broadened to take account of more 'naturalistic' styles of interaction.

The main aim of this work was to arrive at a dialogue design that caters for what people actually say in a particular context, rather than forcing, encouraging, or guiding users into an unnatural interaction style. This reflects the limitations of using speech output to inform users of permitted styles of interaction, and the fact that the user population was intended to be the public at large, thus no specialist knowledge could be assumed.

Three main studies were carried out. In the first, using a slightly controlled, and thus somewhat artificial, setting we captured the behaviour of human information providers and enquirers when information requests to be made were specified to the enquirers. The specification of enquiries was fairly loose, being in the form of scenario-type descriptions, and this study involved calls to a range of information providers, as shown below. All calls were recorded on tape for later analysis.

The following are examples of the tasks given to our volunteer subjects during the initial behavioural study of travel information requests.

(1)　You are in Brighton. You will be travelling to Cardiff from Brighton to attend a meeting on Saturday. You will have to arrive early in the evening on Friday and stay the night. You will need to find out: (i) train and bus times that will suit your needs; (ii) details of suitable overnight accommodation in Cardiff.

> Telephone: Brighton bus information
> Brighton train information
> Cardiff tourist information

(2)　You are in Doncaster. You intend to travel to Peterborough to visit a friend this evening, and you thought you might go to see a film together. Find out firstly what trains and buses will get you to Peterborough by six o'clock.

> Telephone: Doncaster bus information
> Doncaster train information

(3)　You are in Cardiff, and discover you have to go to Liverpool urgently. Find out details of coaches going this afternoon and this evening. Then find out whether it will be cheaper to book a seat through the travel agent in Liverpool than through the one in Cardiff. You will also need to find out details of accommodation available in Liverpool this evening, in case you have to stay the night.

> Telephone: Cardiff travel agents
> Liverpool travel agents
> Liverpool tourist information.

The recordings were transcribed and subjected to fairly informal analysis; the main foci of interest being the nature of the phrases used by callers to specify their enquiry, the points in the dialogue at which important information was provided, and how the conversational strategies adopted by one party affected those adopted by the other. One outcome of this analysis is illustrated in Figure 7.1: a simple description of the stages involved in a typical information request, as identified early in the analysis.

In the second study, we recorded unconstrained human-human conversations in a naturally-occurring question answering context. This was a public information service offering travel timetable details,

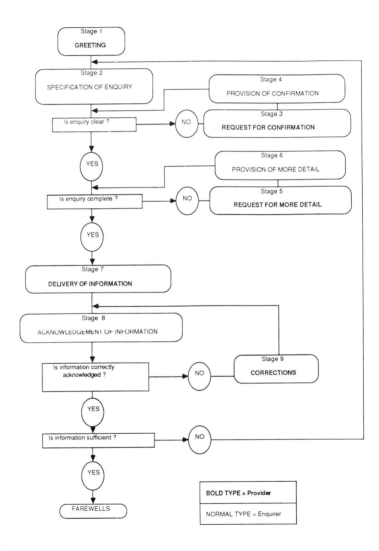

Figure 7.1 - Stages of a Simple Dialogue

closely analogous to the initial target service of the project. We recorded real calls, as they occurred, over a period of several days. The intention was to identify persistent patterns in the way the enquiries, and responses, were phrased, and in the order in which phrases occurred. Recordings were once again transcribed and analysed, looking more closely than in the first study at the phrases actually used, and the order in which items were specified. From this analysis we were able to construct a state diagram showing the course of the interaction between an information seeker and an information provider, on the same topic as our target application. The relative frequencies of occurrence of strategies and phrases were thus derived from naturally-occurring information requests, and this information was then available for programming recognition syntaxes and as a basis for the general dialogue design adopted for VODIS.

Finally, we examined the effect on enquirer responses of varying system behaviour at crucial points in the dialogue, by simulating the strategies of information providers identified from the first two studies. In this case, subjects once again made enquiries as specified by scenarios. Recognition and synthesis capabilities were simulated, and enquiries to the simulated system were made by telephone. All enquiries were recorded and timed. Analysis was in terms of the number of occasions on which enquiries were successful in obtaining the required information, the length of time taken to complete each enquiry, and the nature of the questions and utterances by the enquirer which our simulated system was not able to adequately deal with. The dialogue structure was generally successful, and following amendments in the light of observed inadequacies, permitted a finalisation of the dialogue design for the initial service to be offered by VODIS.

Figure 7.2 provides a short example of a possible VODIS dialogue. Upper-case text indicates voice prompts delivered by the system to the user, lower-case enboldened text are the user's responses. Italicised text, enclosed within square brackets, illustrates the items of information passed to the dialogue controller from the speech recogniser.

Main Findings

Clearly, any interactive information provider, whether human or machine, should always indicate what has been understood to be the details of a query. This gives the user confidence that his request has been understood (if it has), and allows error correction (if it has not). The problem is to find the optimum way of achieving this confirmation/correction for a system with less-than-human speech recognition capability.

Which train do you require ?

I want to go from Ipswich to London on Tuesday.

(to-LONDON/TUESDAY)   **To London on Tuesday ?**

Yes.

(YES) Where are you travelling from ?

From Ipswich.

(from-NORWICH)   **Norwich .**

No, Ipswich.

(from-IPSWICH)   **Ipswich ?**

Yes.

Which train ?	= VODIS
To London.	= Enquirer
(from-NORWICH)	= Recogniser output

About what time do you want to travel ?

Tuesday morning at about 10.

(TUESDAY/10/A.M.)   **Ten in the morning.**

Yes.

(YES) **Trains from Ipswich to London on Tuesday morning:**
Leave Ipswich at 9.41, arrive London Liverpool Street at 10.50,
Leave Ipswich at 10.11, arrive London Liverpool Street at 11.20.
Is that alright ?

When's the next one ?

(NEXT) **Leave Ipswich at 10.41, arrive London, Liverpool Street at 11.50.**
Is that OK ?

Yes, that's fine.

(YES) **Thank you for calling, goodbye.**

Figure 7.2 - VODIS Dialogue Example

The main question is the manner in which the system provides feedback on what has been recognised, given that between one and
several significant items of information may be incorporated in a

user's utterance; and all, none, or some of those items might be correctly recognised.

The 3 studies briefly outlined above allowed us to identify conversational confirmation, correction, and repair strategies appropriate to our target application. Our general strategy, based on a hierarchy of interaction levels approach (Waterworth, 1982), was successfully validated, and the basic dialogue to be tested in later, detailed user trials was established.

Figure 7.3 illustrates confirmation, correction, and repair strategies in a general way. A request can convey information relative to one or more information goals (the goals the system needs to satisfy so that it can answer a query). Information goals are linked when they refer to related topics. Information goals tend to be specified in a particular order when an information request is made. This obviously assists in specifying predictive syntaxes for speech recognition. When goals are sought by the system, because they have not been supplied or identified from a user's volunteered utterances, they are also requested in this order. Once an item of information has been confirmed it is not reconfirmed if offered again. A recognised item that is disconfirmed becomes unrecognised, but will only be sought a limited number of times before remedial action ('repair') is taken. This usually consists of falling back to default assumptions based on the most probable request items, combined with a reduced specificity of information provision. In the most serious cases the dialogue will restart from scratch, or will be transferred to a human operator.

The dialogue design suggested embodies the following rules derived from the conversational analyses:

(1) Request items are offered by the information provider, for confirmation or correction, as they are received (both in manner - grouped or singly - and in time).

(2) There is an upper limit on the number of items that are offered for confirmation or correction together (usually three).

(3) Only items on related topics (information goals) are offered for confirmation or correction together.

(4) Particularly important or doubtful items are offered individually.

(5) Confirmation and the volunteering of further information (relevant to different information goals) tend to be combined.

(6) Volunteered further information tends to be relevant to a topic related to the item(s) offered for confirmation or correction.

(7) Disconfirmation and error correction, by the enquirer, are always combined.

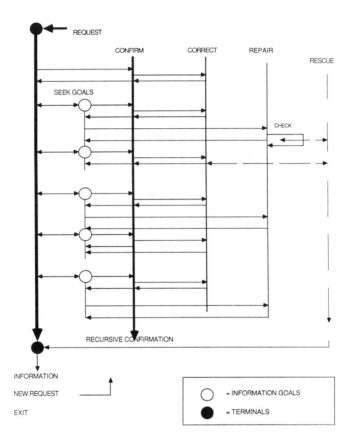

Figure 7.3 - Confirming, Correcting, and Repairing

(8)   Enquiry details requested by the information provider take pre-
       cedence over volunteered details. (This was not derived from
       the behavioural studies, but was necessary to limit the recogni-
       tion vocabulary at certain points of the interaction.)

Discussion

One conclusion from this study is that premature specification of
dialogue strategies is not appropriate to 'naturalistic' interaction with
untrained users. We also confirmed that Conversational Analysis provides a means of identifying the way in which conversational functions

are achieved in practice. As suggested earlier, an approach drawing on the Conversational Analysis tradition is more appropriate than the Discourse Analytic orientation of recent work on quasi-natural language interaction.

This is not to say that there is not a limited set of identifiable 'speech acts' that are performed in conversational behaviour, both between people and between humans and computers (Waterworth, 1982). Rather, it is suggested that the way in which conversational behaviour is used to achieve such underlying functions can only be identified by looking at actual conversations in settings closely analogous to the target application. While some general features of conversational strategies can be identified and applied independently of the application, their realisation in a particular situation varies with discourse topic.

It is important to bear in mind that people do not necessarily respond to machines in the same way as they do to other humans, even when both types of information provider use the same prompting strategies (Underwood & Richards, 1984). It is thus necessary to validate any model derived from the analysis of human-human interaction in a specific human-computer context. An important factor here is likely to be the extent to which the synthesis device used matches the context-dependent prosodic nuances of a human speaker. Although the third study tested our model with a mechanical-sounding voice, further trials with the actual text-to-speech device to be used for the project will be necessary.

The corpus of naturally-occurring information requests we collected has already been used in studies of turn taking (Stephens & Beattie, 1986). One finding from this work was that, in general, subjects needed to hear the utterances of information providers, not merely read a verbatim transcript, to be able to distinguish between turn-final and turn-medial utterances. For most speakers, they needed the prosodic cues available in recordings, but absent from the transcripts. However, they were able to do without this information in the case of one particular provider. It appeared that subjects did this on the basis of certain combinations of topic (e.g. time or cost of travel) and mode of expression (e.g. 'impersonal' or 'personal'). Studies such as this are important to us because of the light they shed on possible ways of signalling to users that an information-providing system is expecting a response and, reciprocally, of interpreting when users have finished their turn and expect a response from the system.

A more detailed exploration of certain aspects of confirmation and correction for speech recognising systems is described below.

7.3.2.2. Experiment: How and when should feedback be provided?

This study examined three main questions. What is the best modality for presenting feedback with a voice recognition system; specifically, visual versus auditory? Secondly, what is the best method of entering, and of confirming and correcting, items of information by voice; global versus piecemeal? Finally, does the effect of specification strategy interact with the number of items of information to be entered, confirmed, or corrected?

The task for the experiment was the voice control of an electronic video cassette recorder. Forty-eight subjects each attempted to set up the device to record particular video programmes 40 times, making 1600 attempts in all. The number of items of relevant items of information they had to specify by voice was either 2 (channel and time), 3 (channel, time and day) or 4 (channel, time, day, and period of day). Four methods of data entry, confirmation and correction were compared. These were (i) global entry, global confirmation/correction; (ii) piecemeal entry, global confirmation/correction; (iii) global entry, piecemeal confirmation/correction, and (iv) piecemeal entry, piecemeal confirmation/correction. 'Global' specification of items refers to the case where all items are specified at one go, without intervening feedback. 'Piecemeal' specification refers to the case where each item is specified individually. Feedback was always terminal, i.e. all items of the task were specified (by whichever method) before feedback, leading on to confirmation or correction, was offered.

Following a practice session, all subjects performed half the tasks with auditory feedback, and half with visual. Half the subjects experienced auditory feedback first, for the other half the order was reversed. Number of items to be specified was a between-subjects variable; one third of subjects always specified 2 items, one third always specified 3 items, and the remainder always specified 4 items.

A speech recogniser was not used for this experiment; recogniser performance was simulated such that each subject was 'misrecognised' on 20% of utterances, balanced across experimental conditions. The time taken to speak the words needed to complete each transaction with the system was recorded, so that average transaction times for each condition could be calculated.

Results and Discussion

An Analysis of Variance was used to test the significance of the transaction time results obtained. There was no significant difference in transaction times as a function of feedback modality; the means were 9.31 s for visual, and 9.05 s for auditory. This seems to contradict the 'Stimulus-Central Processing-Response Compatibility Model' of Wickens and Vidulich (1982) which suggests that performance will be best if visual feedback follows manual entry and auditory feedback follows speech input. However, although performance was not significantly affected by feedback modality, 65% of subjects preferred auditory feedback, as indicated by questionnaire responses. The main reason given for this expressed preference was that auditory feedback seemed quicker; others included the observation that spoken feedback was less impersonal than visually presented feedback, and that checking for errors was less demanding.

Not surprisingly, overall transaction time increased with the number of items to be specified although, again not surprisingly, transaction time per item of information decreased with the number of items to be specified. Three and four items were not different from each other in this respect, however, perhaps because time and period are so closely bound together as to be associated in subjects' minds and in practice. The interaction between feedback modality and number of items to be specified was not significant.

Of more interest is the effect of data entry and confirmation/correction strategy, which was highly significant. Global specification and global confirmation/correction resulted in the shortest overall transaction times across all numbers of items (mean = 7.28 s). Piecemeal specification combined with global confirmation/correction resulted in a mean overall transaction time of 8.58 s, whereas for global specification with piecemeal confirmation/correction the value was 9.88 s. The least efficient combination was piecemeal specification with piecemeal confirmation/correction (10.98 s). A Duncan's Multiple Range Test indicated that each of these means was significantly different from all the others. Subjects' opinion, as assessed by questionnaire, confirmed the superiority of the global entry, global confirmation/correction combination. This was the method of choice for 90% of all subjects. It will be remembered that recogniser error rate was fixed at 20% of utterances. It is likely that the most efficient combination of strategies, as regards error correction, will depend on recognition accuracy. Further experimentation could test this possibility, which was not addressed by the present experiment. It seems likely, however, that for error rates of up to 20%, global entry and confirmation correction is to be preferred, subject to the effect of the number of items to be specified (see below).

The interaction between specification methods and number of items to be specified was also significant. This was such that the difference between strategies, as described above, increased as the number of items to be specified increased. It might have been expected that as the number of items increased the relative efficiency of the global-global combination would be moderated. Certainly, the findings from the study reported in Part 1 indicated that no more than 3 items would normally be combined globally in human-human exchanges. However, the differences in performance between 3 and 4 items were not significant, so the two results are not directly in conflict. Further experimentation may reveal such a limit with a greater number of items than was used here, but the present results provide no evidence that this might be the case. On the contrary, the trend would suggest that the relative benefit of the preferred combination would increase as the number of items to be specified increased. Similarly, it might have been expected that preferred modality of feedback would be a function of number of items specified, specification method, or both, but both these interactions were nonsignificant. Again, further research looking at the specification of larger numbers of items may reveal such an effect, but there is no evidence for such an expectation in the present results.

The results of this experiment suggest that, for the task examined here, i.e. the vocal specification of up to 4 items of information, feedback modality will not affect performance, although auditory feedback will be preferred to visual. The most efficient method of item specification was global data entry combined with global confirmation/correction. There is a need for further studies of this type, looking at different types of information specification task, at the specification of larger numbers of items, and examining the effects of recognition accuracy.

7.3.2.3. Observational and experimental studies of interactive behaviour

The two types of study described above illustrate two different, and, I believe, complementary, approaches to identifying suitable interactive strategies for human-computer interaction by voice. Both types of study are necessary, for the following reasons. The first allows strategies to be identified that will seem natural to users of systems, on the basis of human-human information query exchanges. However, it is not yet possible to fully duplicate human performance because of technological constraints on the capabilities of speech synthesisers and recognisers. Detailed experimentation is needed, in addition to such observational analysis, to address particular aspects of the interactive situation, reflecting these technological limitations and the fact that not all human-computer interactions have a direct analogue in human-human conversation. The main findings from the first type of study are quite generalisable, although details of interactive strategies will vary, as already suggested, with discourse topic. The results of the second type of study are more restricted in applicability, and many such studies will be needed to gain detailed knowledge of preferred methods of interaction across a range of tasks and technological implementations.

8

Conclusions

8.1. THE STATE OF THE ART

Systems which are, at least partially, conversational in nature, are already appearing. We have seen that interaction with machines, by means of spoken and written language, is becoming increasingly common in a range of situations including consumer products, office systems, and for various general- and special-purpose telecommunications applications (notably information access). Because text-to-speech synthesis is so flexible, it is increasingly being used as a means of presenting information to users of advanced computerised systems. Applications include voice output for a range of interactive information services, database enquiry, and electronic mail interrogation. Similarly, word-based speech recognition technology has begun to make an impact in the market place, although within a relatively restricted range of applications. Interaction via written language includes text scanning, understanding, and generation. Applications to date have been predominantly in the areas of database access, and text editing and creation systems. Gradually, the technologies of speech, and natural-language interaction, are converging through the development of 'conversational systems'. We have outlined some of the work involved in this development process; including psychological studies of synthetic speech perception and the use of recognition, linguistic work on the way functions are achieved through language, behavioural studies of how such functions are achieved in practice, and AI issues of how conversational dialogues can best be represented within computer systems.

As yet, the users of conversational systems must work harder at the interaction process than is ideal. The technology of speech attempts, to varying levels of detail, to duplicate human capacities for speech interpretation and production. As yet, however, all such implementations fall short of realising this aim fully. The limitations of the technology emphasise the need for sound psychological research to maximise the effectiveness of systems at their current level of development. As we saw in Chapter 2, the fundamental problem with current speech synthesis is the inadequate specification of acoustic cues to phonetic segments. This results in more effort being allocated by listeners to encoding than is the case with natural speech. Because capacity is limited, this allocation of resources to encoding is at the expense of rehearsing previously-encoded items. One simple way of improving memory for synthetically-presented material, to compensate for this impairment (pending the development of improved text-to-speech implementations), is to insert exaggerated pauses at syntactic boundary points in sentences, or between groups of a few items when presenting lists.

The traffic between the psychology and the technology of speech recognition has been two-way. Initially, work looking at the way people might interpret spoken language preceded practical developments in machine recognition. As the availability of relatively cheap processing power increased, attention focussed on implementations of recognition techniques, with behavioural research continuing in parallel, and largely independently. A truly symbiotic relationship has developed between the two disciplines in the case of recognition, and this is beginning to develop for synthesis, too.

In psychology, a view of memory involving context-sensitive, associative coding, implemented on highly parallel and distributed systems, is currently attracting considerable interest. Attempts to achieve human-like performance, by machine, on perceptual tasks such as speech recognition has led to the reinstatement of what was a largely discounted approach to human cognition. In Artificial Intelligence, the idea of duplicating human performance at the neuronal level was popular in the 1960s, but was dropped because of the limited capacities of the machines at the time. With the development of relatively cheap, large, computer memories, the 'neural net' approach has been resurrected as a feasible model of human visual and auditory perception, and one that may overcome the limits in performance that other approaches seem to have reached. Thus, attempts to implement human-like skills within computer systems have led to revisions and development of psychological theory, and of notions of machine intelligence.

Despite this cross-fertilisation of psychology and artificial intelligence, we saw in Chapter 3 that the truly conversational computer is much less a reality than is widely thought. Although it was predicted a decade ago that speech input and output (I/O) devices would revolutionise the human-computer interface, allowing unrestricted, virtually error-free input and retrieval of data - possibly even automatic, speech-driven dictation of letters and documents - speech is still only being used in a few, select applications. Much of the reason for this is that the performance levels of speech I/O devices have not improved in accordance with predictions. However, it is also likely that certain groups who could benefit from using the technology are actually deterred from doing so by the fact that they do not know what it can offer them. Scepticism is created by the distinct lack of objective and universal performance measures which exist for speech I/O devices. An improvement on available evaluation techniques for synthetic speech was outlined in Chapter 4, based on the time taken for listeners to process speech tokens. Chapter 5 discussed techniques for achieving improved performance from existing recognition hardware, by making the system adapt to changes in the speaker's voice (unsuccessful), and through improved recogniser 'training regimes' (successful, but only for female speakers).

8.2. THE FUTURE

Technical advances will no doubt improve recognition and synthesis in the future. As already pointed out, this is likely to involve more closely modelling human perceptual and production skills. But producing recognition and synthesis devices, however excellent, will not be sufficient to bring about the successful development of conversational systems. Systems need to operate at the level of *discourse*; language is neither produced nor understood in a vacuum, the context in which sentences are produced or received is the key to its meaning.

Despite reservations about the notion of 'Speech Acts', it was suggested in Chapter 6 that the idea of of utterances reflecting a limited set of underlying functions that speakers are attempting to achieve, is likely to prove useful in the realm of human-computer interaction. But account must be taken of situation-specific knowledge about how 'speech events' are used to perform dialogue acts. Such inferencing behaviour is necessary to identify speech events in particular contexts. We have suggested more than once that the way in which conversational behaviour is used to achieve underlying functions can only be identified by looking at actual conversations in particular settings. We also suggested that the separation of information flow between the system and user (the dialogue), from underlying task execution (the application) makes dialogue decisions much easier to implement and test. The decisions to be made cover the style of the interaction and the actual content of the dialogue, in terms of information conveyed and interpreted, and the allocation and flow of control between system and user. Dialogue specification tools, which allow the rapid and convenient prototyping of potential conversational dialogue structures, are likely to proliferate in the next few years. These are a practical embodiment of the 'separable user interface' philosophy.

Interfaces that handle a small set of 'naturalish' language have been appearing gradually over the last few years, in areas where relatively simple techniques can yield dividends. They can be seen as early steps towards conversational interfaces, although little has much been done to make such interfaces truly natural, in the sense of similarity to human-human linguistic behaviour. Chapter 7 described the sort of studies that are needed to achieve genuinely conversational interaction. We suggested that the way in which conversational behaviour is used to achieve information exchange, including the control of the dialogue itself, can only be identified by looking at actual conversations in settings closely analogous to the target application. While some general features of conversational strategies can be identified and applied independently of the application, their realisation in a particular situation varies with discourse topic. Detailed experimental studies, with the recognition and synthesis devices to be used for a particular application, are also necessary.

To be successful, research into the development of conversational systems must avoid two pitfalls; of either concentrating exclusively on the *form* the dialogue representation takes, or of considering the *content* of actual dialogues without gaining an understanding of the ways in which such information could be implemented in an intelligent system. The former is true of most AI work in the area, where scant attention is directed towards accurately identifying the behavioural strategies to be modelled, and of experimentally assessing the success (or otherwise) of resulting dialogue schemes. AI systems, however good their architecture, and whatever their potential for intelligent behaviour through the representation of appropriate knowledge, do not of themselves guarantee good communicative behaviour with their users. Such behaviour depends, of course, on knowledge about appropriate interactive strategies being programmed into them, and on the success of the resulting dialogues being tested in a rigorous way. This dimension has been sadly lacking in the largely ad hoc development of intelligent systems to date. The latter criticism applies to behavioural work on language and human-computer dialogues that neglects to consider the ways in which dialogues may be implemented in actual interactive systems. Such approaches lack insights into the emerging possibilities of intelligent systems, specifically the ways in which behavioural knowledge can be used in actual implementations.

Conversational interfaces are of potential use in a wide range of applications. To be successful they must be restricted to limited topic domains. We have suggested that the best way to go about deciding on the dialogue structure for such conversational interactions is to study and model the way in which human information query conversations, on similarly restricted topics, are conducted in life. Elements of linguistic theory, knowledge representation and conversational analysis, and the knowledge and experience gained in evaluating alternative approaches in practice, are essential to the successful development of interactive systems in the future. Such work can also form the basis for the development of techniques for automating the processes of collecting and analysing behavioural data, and of implementing dialogues based on this information quickly and intelligibly, using appropriate interface development tools. Techniques for processing spoken and written natural language will not realise their full potential, in the design of enhanced interactive systems, unless knowledge gained from the analysis of human use of language is incorporated in their development.

References

Ainsworth, W.A. (1976) - 'Mechanisms of Speech Recognition'. Oxford: Pergamon.

Allen, J. (1980) - 'Speech Synthesis from Text'. In J.C. Simon (ed). 'Spoken Language Generation and Understanding'. Dordrecht, Holland: Reidel.

Allen, J. (1983) - 'Recognizing intentions from natural language utterances'. In Brady, M., & Berwick, R. C. (eds) - 'Computational Models of Discourse'. Cambridge, Massachusetts: MIT.

Allport, D.A. (1980) - 'Attention and Performance'. In Claxton, G. (ed) - 'Cognitive Psychology: New Directions'. London: Routledge and Kegan Paul.

Alterman, R. (1986) - 'Summarization in the Small'. In Sharkey, N. E. (ed) - 'Advances in Cognitive Science 1'. Chichester: Ellis Horwood.

Alty, J.L. - 'The Application of Path Algebras to Interactive Dialogue Design'. In 'Proceedings of The User Interface: The Ergonomics of Interactive Computing'. Ergonomics Society Conference, Leicester Polytechnic, September 1983.

Anderson, R.C. (1977) - 'The Notion of Schemata and the Educational Enterprise'. In Anderson, R. C., Spiro, R. J., & Montague, W. E. (eds) - 'Schooling and the Acquisition of Knowledge'. Hillsdale, New Jersey: Erlbaum.

Arnott, J.L. and Newell, A.F. (1984) 'Stenotype Shorthand and Speech Synthesis in Vocal Prosthesis for the Dextrous Speech Impaired'. In 'Proceedings of the 2nd International Conference on Rehabilitation Engineering'. Ottawa: The Rehabilitation Society.

Austin, J.L. (1962) - 'How To Do Things With Words'. Oxford: Oxford University Press.

Barr, A., & Feigenbaum, E.A. (eds) (1981) - 'The Handbook of Artificial Intelligence: Volume I'. London: Pitman.

Barry, W.J. (1984) - 'Segment or Syllable ? A Reaction Time Investigation of Phonetic Processing'. Language and Speech, 27, 1-15.

Bateman, R.F. - 'A translator to encourage user modifiable man-machine dialog'. In M. E. Sime & M. J. Coombs (eds) - 'Designing for human-computer communication'. London: Academic, 1983.

Beattie, G.W., Cutler, A., & Pearson, M. (1982) - 'Why is Mrs Thatcher Interrupted so often ?'. Nature, 300, 744-747.

Bennett, R.W. & Lincoln, C.E. (1985) - 'Measuring the Quality of Voice Circuits for Telecommunications Applications'. In 'Proceedings of the 11th International Symposium on Human Factors in Telecommunications'. Cesson Sevigne: CCETT.

Berman, J.V.F. (1984) - 'Speech Technology in a High Workload Environment'. In 'Proceedings of the First International Conference on Speech Technology'. Bedford: IFS Publications.

Bever, T.G., Lackner, J., & Kirk, R. (1969) - 'The Underlying Structure Sentence is the Primary Unit of Immediate Speech Processing'. Perception and Psychophysics, 5, 225-234.

Bobrow, D.G., & Collins, A. (eds) (1975) - 'Representation and Understanding'. Orlando, Florida: Academic.

Bobrow, D.G. & Winograd, T. (1977) - 'An overview of KRL, a Knowledge Representation Language'. Cognitive Science, 1, (1).

Bobrow, D.G., Kaplan, R.M., Kay, M., Norman, D.A., Thompson, H., & Winograd, T. (1977) - 'GUS, A Frame-Driven Dialog System'. Artificial Intelligence, 8, 155-173.

Bolinger, D. (1972) - 'Accent is predictable (if you're a mind reader)'. Language, 83, 633-644.

Bridle, J.S. & Ralls, M.P. (1985) - 'An approach to speech recognition using synthesis-by-rule'. In F. Fallside & W. A. Woods (eds), 'Computer Speech Processing'. Englewood Cliffs, NJ: Prentice/Hall.

Broadbent, D.E. (1958) - 'Perception and Communication'. Oxford: Pergamon.

Broadbent, D.E., Fitzgerald, P. & Broadbent, M.H.P. (1986) - 'Implicit and explicit knowledge in the control of complex systems'. British Journal of Psychology, 77, 33-50.

Brown, G., & Yule, G. (1983) - 'Discourse Analysis'. Cambridge: Cambridge University Press.

CCITT [International Consultative Committee on Telegraphy and

Telephony] (1980) - 'Methods used for Assessing Telephony Transmission Performance'. Yellow Book, Vol. 5.

Chomsky, N. (1957) - 'Syntactic Structures'. The Hague: Mouton.

Chomsky, N. & Miller, G.A. (1963) - 'Introduction to the Formal Analysis of Natural Languages'. In R.D. Luce, R.R. Bush. & E. Galanter (eds), ' Handbook of Mathematical Psychology'. New York: Wiley.

Clark, H., & Haviland, S.E. (1977) - 'Comprehension and the Given-New Contract'. In Freedle, R. (ed) - 'Discourse Production and Comprehension'. Hillsdale, New Jersey: Erlbaum.

Cockton, G. - 'Dialogue Management Systems'. Presentation at the Heriot-Watt/Strathclyde MMI Unit Research Workshop No. 1, April 1985.

Cody, P.C. & Smith, J.K. (1984) - 'Applied Statistics and the SAS Programming Language'. Amsterdam: North Holland.

Cohen, P. R. & Feigenbaum, E.A. (eds) (1982) - 'The Handbook of Artificial Intelligence: Volume III'. London: Pitman.

Cole, R.A. (ed) (1980) - 'Perception and Production of Fluent Speech'. Hillsdale, NJ: Erlbaum.

Cole, R.A. & Jakimik, J. (1978) - 'Understanding Speech: How Words are Heard'. In Underwood, G. (ed) 'Strategies of Information Processing'. London, Academic Press.

Cole, R.A. & Jakimik, J. (1980) - 'A Model of Speech Perception'. In Cole (1980).

Cole, R.A. & Scott, B. (1974) - 'Towards a Theory of Speech Perception'. Psychological Review, 81, 348-374.

Cole, R.A., Rudnicky, R.I., Zue, V.W., & Reddy, D.R. (1980) - 'Speech as Patterns on Paper'. In Cole (1980).

Conolly, D.W. (1977) - 'Voice Data Entry in Air Traffic Control'. Paper presented at the Conference on Voice Technology for Interactive Real Time Control Systems Applications. NASA Ames Research Centre, California.

Corkhill, D. (1979) - 'Hierarchical Planning in a Distributed Environment'. Technical Report 12, DOC, University of Massachusetts, USA.

Craik, F.I.M., & Lockhart, R.S. (1972) - 'Levels of processing: a framework for memory research'. Journal of Verbal Learning and Verbal Behavior, 11, 671-684.

Cutler, A. (1977) - 'The context dependence of "intonational meanings"'. Chicago Linguistic Society Papers, 13, 104-115.

Cutler, A. & Foss, D.J. (1977) - 'On the Role of Sentence Stress in Sentence Processing'. Language and Speech, 20, 1-10.

Dallett, K.M. (1964) - 'Intelligibility and short-term memory in the repetition of digit strings'. Journal of Speech and Hearing Research, 7, 362-368.

Damper, R.I. (1984) - 'Voice Input Aids for the Physically Disabled'. International Journal of Man-Machine Studies, Vol. 21, 6, 541-553.

Damper, R.I. & McDonald, S. L. (1984) - 'Template Adaptation in Speech Recognition'. Proceedings of the Institute of Acoustics, 6, (4), 293-300.

DeGeorge, M. (1981) - 'Experiments in Automatic Speech Verification'. Paper presented at Carnham Conference on Crime Countermeasures, Levington, Kentucky. Reprinted in Electronic Engineering, June, 1981, pp 73-83.

Dell, G.S. & Newman, J.E. (1978) - 'Detecting phonemes in fluent speech'. Austin, Texas: Psychonomic Association.

Deutsch, J.A. & Deutsch, D. (1963) - 'Attention: Some Theoretical Considerations'. Psychological Review, 70, 80-90.

Dilts, M. (1984) - 'Text to Speech'. In G. Bristow (ed), 'Electronic Speech Synthesis'. London: Granada.

Edman, T.R. & Metz, S.V. (1983) - 'Methodology for the Evaluation of Real-time Speech Digitization'. In 'Proceedings of the Human Factors Society 27th Annual Meeting'. The Human Factors Society, Santa Monica, California.

Edmonds, E.A. (1978) - 'Adaptable man/machine interfaces for complex dialogues'. In 'Proceedings of the European Computing Congress', London, pp 639-646.

Edmonds, E.A. (1981) - 'Adaptive man-computer interfaces'. In M. J. Coombs & J. L. Alty (eds) 'Computing Skills and the User Interface'. London: Academic.

Edmonds, E.A. (1982) - 'The man-computer interface: a note on concepts and design'. International Journal of Man-Machine Studies, 16, 231-236.

Edmonds, E., Guest, S., & Pollard, A. (1984) - 'SYNICS1.5 User Guide'. Human-Computer Interface Research Unit, Leicester Polytechnic.

Ehrlich, W.R. & Williges, R.C. (eds) (1986) - 'Human-Computer Dialogue Design'. Amsterdam: Elsevier.

Elman, J.L. & McClelland, J.L. (1985) - 'An Architecture for Parallel Processing in Speech Recognition'. In Schroeder (1985).

Erlman, L.D. & Lesser, V.R. (1980) - 'The Hearsay-II Speech Understanding System: A Tutorial'. In Lea, W. A. (ed) - 'Trends In Speech Recognition'. Englewood Cliffs, NJ: Prentice-Hall.

Fallside, F. & Young, S.J. (1984) - 'Speech Output from Complex Systems'. In Bristow, G.(ed), 'Electronic Speech Synthesis'. London: Granada.

Fikes, R. & Nilsson, N. (1971) - 'STRIPS: A New Approach to the Application of Theorem Proving to Problem Solving'. Technical Note 43, SRI International, USA.

Fischer, G., Lemke, A., & Schwab, T. (1985) - 'Knowledge-based Help Systems'. In 'Proceedings of CHI'85 - Conference on Human Factors in Computing Systems'. Association for Computing Machinery, New York. (Published in Europe as L.Borman and B.Curtis (eds) - 'Human Factors in Computing Systems II'. Amsterdam: North-Holland.)

Fodor, J.A., Bever, T.G. & Garrett, M.F. (1974) - 'The Psychology of Language'. New York: McGraw-Hill.

Foss, D.J. (1969) - 'Decision Processes During Sentence Comprehension: Effects of Lexical Item Difficulty and Position upon Decision Times'. Journal of Verbal Learning and Verbal Behaviour, 8, 457-462.

Fourcin, A.J. (1975) - 'Speech perception in the absence of speech productive ability'. In 'Language and Cognitive Deficits and Retardation'. London: Butterworth.

Fourcin, A.J. & Lennenberg, E. (1973) - 'Language development in the absence of expressive speech'. In 'Foundations of Language Development'. IBRO-UNESCO.

Fowler, C.A., Rubin, P., Remez, R.E. & Turvey, M.T. (1980) - 'Implications For Speech Production of a General Theory of Action'. In Butterworth, B. (ed), 'Language Production'. London: Academic Press, 373-420.

Fum, D., Guido, G., & Tasso, C. (1985) - 'Evaluating Importance: A Step Towards Summarisation'. Proceedings 9th IJCAI, LA, August.

Goodman, G., & Reddy, R. (1980) - 'Alternative Control Structures for Speech Understanding Systems'. In Lea (1980).

Gould, J.D., Conti, J. & Hovanyecz, T. (1982) - 'Composing Letters with a Simulated Listening Typewriter'. In 'Proceedings of the Conference on Human Factors in Computer Systems', Gaithersberg, Maryland, USA. The Human Factors Society, Santa Monica, California.

Green, T.R.G. & Clark, G. (1981) - 'Checkout: Heuristics Speechlink'. Personal Computer World, June, 1981.

Green, T.R.G., Payne, S.J., Morrison, D.L. & Shaw, A. (1983) - 'Friendly Interfacing to Simple Speech Recognisers'. Behaviour and Information Technology, Vol. 2, 1, 23-28.

Grice, H.P. (1975) - 'Logic and conversation'. In Cole, P., & Morgan, J. L. (eds) - 'Syntax and Semantics 3: Speech Acts'. New York: Academic.

Grice, H.P. (1978) - 'Further notes on logic and conversation'. In Cole, P. (ed) - 'Syntax and Semantics 9: Pragmatics'. New York: Academic.

Grosjean, F. (1979) - 'Spoken word recognition and the gating paradigm'. Unpublished manuscript, Northeast University.

Guest, S.P. (1982) - 'The use of tools for dialogue design'. International Journal of Man-Machine Studies, 16, 263-285.

Haggard, M., Ambler, S. & Callow, M. (1970) - 'Pitch as a Voicing Cue'. Journal of the Acoustical Society of America, 47, 613-617.

Halle, M. & Keyser, S.J.(1971) - 'English Stress'. New York: Harper and Row.

Hanley, J.R. & Thomas, A. (1984) - 'Maintenance rehearsal and the articulatory loop'. British Journal of Psychology, 75, 521-527.

Hartson, H.R. & Johnson, D.H. (1983) - 'Dialogue Management: New Concepts in Human-Computer Interface Development'.

Technical Report CSIE-83-13, Office of Naval Research, Code 442, 800 North Quincy Street, Arlington VA 22217, USA.

Hayes, P.J. (1984) - 'Executable Interface Definitions Using Form-Based Interface Abstractions'. In 'Advances in Computer-Human Interaction', H. R. Hartson (ed). New Jersey: Ablex.

Hayes, P.J., Szekely, P.A. & Lerner, R.A. (1985) - 'Design Alternatives for User Interface Management Systems Based on Experience with COUSIN'. In 'Proceedings of CHI'85 - Conference on Human Factors in Computing Systems'. Association for Computing Machinery, New York. (Published in Europe as L.Borman and B.Curtis (eds) - 'Human Factors in Computing Systems II'. Amsterdam: North-Holland.)

Hayes-Roth, B. (1980) - 'Human Planning Processes'. Report No. R-2670-ONR, Rand Corporation, Santa Monica, California.

Henderson, L. (1982) - 'Orthography and Word Recognition in Reading'. London: Academic.

Hinton, G.E. & Anderson, J.A. (1981) - 'Parallel models of associative memory'. Hillsdale, NJ: Erlbaum.

IBM (1983) - 'Interactive System Productivity Facility: General Information'. IBM Publication Number GC34-2078-2.

Johnson, T. (1985) - 'Natural Language Computing: the Commercial Applicatons'. London: Ovum.

Johnson-Laird, P.N. (1981) - 'Mental Models of Meaning'. In Joshi et al. (1981).

Joshi, A.K., Webber, B.L., & Sag, I.A. (eds) (1981) - 'Elements of Discourse Understanding'. Cambridge: Cambridge University Press.

Kintsch, W. (1974) - 'The Representation of Meaning in Memory'. Hillsdale, NJ: Erlbaum.

Klatt, D.H. (1980) - 'Speech perception: A Model of Acoustic-Phonetic Analysis and Lexical Access'. In Cole (1980).

Kuipers, B.J. (1975) - 'A Frame for Frames: Representing Knowledge for Recognition'. In Bobrow and Collins (1975).

Lea, W.A. (1980) - 'Trends in Speech Recognition'. Englewood Cliffs, New Jersey: Prentice-Hall.

Lehnert, W.G. (1978) - 'The Process of Question Answering'. Hillsdale, New Jersey: Erlbaum.

Lehnert, W.G. (1981) - 'A Computational theory of human question answering'. In Joshi et al. (1981).

Levinson, S.C. (1983) - 'Pragmatics'. Cambridge: Cambridge University Press.

Levinson, S.E. & Shipley, K.L. (1980) - 'A Conversational-Mode Airline Information and Reservation System Using Speech Input and Output'. Bell System Technical Journal, 59, 119-137.

Levitt, H., Pickett, R.M. and Houde, R.A. (1980) - 'Sensory Aids for the Hearing Impaired'. IEEE Press, New York.

Liberman, A.M., Cooper, F.S., Shankweiler, D.P., & Studdert-Kennedy, M. (1967) - 'Perception of the Speech Code'. Psychological Review, 74, 431-461.

Luce, P.A., Feustel, J.C., & Pisoni, D.B. (1983) - 'Capacity demands in short-term memory for synthetic and natural speech'. Human Factors, 25, 17-32.

MacNeilage, P.F. (1970) - 'Motor Control of Serial Ordering of Speech'. Psychological Review, 77, 182-196.

MacNeilage, P.F., & MacNeilage, L.A. (1973) - 'Central Processes Controlling Speech Production During Sleep and Waking'. In McGuigan, F.J. & Schoonover, R.A. (eds), 'The Psychophysiology of Thinking'. New York: Academic Press.

Mangione, P.A. (1986) - 'SSI's Phonetic Engine'. In Speech Technology Magazine, Mar/Apr 1986, 84-86.

Marcus, S.M. (1985) - 'Associative Models and the Time Course of Speech'. In Schroeder (1985).

Marslen-Wilson, W.D. (1975) - 'Sentence perception as an interactive parallel process'. Science, 189, 226-228.

Marslen-Wilson, W.D. (1980) - 'Speech understanding as a psychological process'. In J. C.Simon (ed) op cit.

Marslen-Wilson, W. & Tyler, L.K. (1980) - 'The Temporal Structure of Spoken Language Understanding'. Cognition, 8, 1-71.

Marslen-Wilson, W. & Welsh, A. (1978) - 'Processing Interactions and Lexical Access during Word Recognition in Continuous Speech'. Cognitive Psychology, 10, 29-63.

Martin, T.B. & Welch, J.R. (1980) - 'Practical Speech Recognisers and Some Performance Effective Parameters' In Lea (1980).

Mazuryk, G.F., & Lockhart, R.S. (1974) - 'Negative recency and levels of processing'. Canadian Journal of Psychology, 28, 114-123.

Mehler, J. (1981) - 'The role of syllables in speech processing: infant and adult data'. Philosophical Transactions of the Royal Society of London, Series B, 295 (1077), 333-352.

Mellish, C. (1985) - 'Computer Interpretation of Natural Language Descriptions'. Chichester: Ellis Horwood.

Michaelis, P.R. and Wiggins, R.H. (1982) - 'A Human Factors engineer's introduction to speech synthesisers'. In 'Directions in Human-Computer Interaction', Badre, A. and Schneiderman, B. (eds). New Jersey: Ablex.

Michie, D. (1980) - 'Problems of the conceptual interface between machine and human problem solvers'. Experimental Programming Unit Report 36. Edinburgh: Machine Intelligence Research Unit, University of Edinburgh.

Miller, G.A. (1962) - 'Decision Units in the Perception of Speech'. IRE Transactions in Information Theory, 8, 81-83.

Miller, G.A., & Isard, S. (1963) - 'Some perceptual consequences of linguistic rules'. Journal of Verbal Learning and Verbal Behaviour, 2, 217-228.

Miller, G.A., Heise, G.A., & Lichten, W. (1951) - 'The Intelligibility of Speech as a Function of the Context of the Test Materials'. Journal of Experimental Psychology, 41, 329-335.

Minsky, M. (1975) - 'A framework for representing knowledge'. In P. Winston (ed) 'The psychology of computer vision'. New York: McGraw-Hill, pp 211-277.

Moore, R.K. (1977) - 'Evaluating Speech Recognisers'. IEEE transactions on Acoustics, Speech and Signal Processing, 25, (2).

Moore, R.K. (1984) - 'Overview of Speech Input'. Proceedings of 1st International Conference on Speech Technology. Bedford: IFS.

Morton, J. (1981) - 'The status of information processing models of language'. Philosophical Transactions of the Royal Society of London, series B, 295 (1077), 387-396.

Morton, J., & Long, J. (1976) - 'Effect of word transitional probability on phoneme identification'. Journal of Verbal Learning and Verbal Behaviour, 15, 43-51.

Murrell, G.A., & Morton, J. (1974) - 'Word recognition and morphemic structure'. Journal of Experimental Psychology, 102, 963-968.

Newell, A. (1980) - 'Harpy, Production Systems, and Human Cognition'. In Cole (1980).

Nooteboom, S.G. (1983) - 'The temporal organisation of speech and the process of spoken-word recognition'. IPO (Eindhoven) Progress Report, 18, 32-36.

Norman, D.A. (1980) - 'Copycat Science or Does the mind really work by table look-up ?'. In Cole (1980).

Peckham, J.B. (1984) - 'Speech Recognition - What is it worth ?'. In 'Proceedings of the First International Conference on Speech Technology'. Bedford: IFS.

Pisoni, D.B. (1981) - 'Some current theoretical issues in speech perception'. Cognition, 10, 249-259.

Pisoni, D.B. (1981) - 'Speeded Classification of Natural and Synthetic Speech in a Lexical Decision Task'. Journal of the Acoustical Society of America, 70, S98.

Pisoni, D.B., & Hunnicutt, S. (1980) - 'Perceptual evaluation of MITalk: the MIT unrestricted text-to-speech system'. IEEE International conference record on acoustics, speech and signal processing, pp 572-575.

Power, R. (1979) - 'The organisation of purposeful dialogues'. Linguistics, 17, 107-152.

Pratt, R. L. (1981) - 'On the Use of Reaction Time as an Intelligibility Measure'. British Journal of Audiology, 15, 253-255.

Quillian, M. R. (1968) - 'Semantic Memory'. In Minsky, M. (ed) - 'Semantic Information Processing'. Cambridge, Mass.: MIT Press.

Rabbitt, P. (1966) - 'Recognition: Memory for words correctly heard in noise.' Psychonomic Science, 6, 383-384.

Rabbitt, P. (1968) - 'Channel-capacity, intelligibility, and immediate memory'. Quarterly Journal of Experimental Psychology, 20, 241-248.

Reddy, D.R. (1976) - 'Speech recognition by machine: A review'. Proceedings of the IEEE, 64, 501-531.

Reddy, D.R. (1980) - 'Machine Models of Speech Perception'. In Cole (1980).

Redpath, D. (1984) - 'Specific Applications of Speech Synthesis'. In 'Proceedings of the First International Conference on Speech Technology'. Bedford: IFS.

Rehsoft, C. (1984) - 'Voice Recognition at the Ford Warehouse in Cologne'. In 'Proceedings of the First International Conference on Speech Technology'. Bedford: IFS.

Reichman, R. (1985) - 'Getting Computers to Talk Like You and Me'. Cambridge, Mass.: MIT Press.

Richards, M. A., & Underwood, K. (1984) - 'How should people and computers speak to each other ?'. In 'Proceedings of Interact '84 - 1st IFIP Conference on HCI'. Amsterdam: Elsevier.

Rubenstein, H. (1984) - 'Radio Distributed Digital Daily Newspaper for the Blind'. In 'Proceedings of the 2nd International Conference on Rehabilitation Engineering'. Ottawa: The Rehabilitation Society.

Rumelhart, D. (1975) - 'Notes on a Schema for Stories'. In Bobrow and Collins (1975).

Rumelhart, D. (1977) - 'Introduction to human information processing'. New York: Wiley.

Russell, M.J., Moore, R.K., Tomlinson, M.J. & Deacon, J.C.A. (1983) - 'Speech Database Recordings'. London: HMSO.

Sanford, A. J. & Garrod, S.C. (1981) - 'Understanding Written Language'. Chichester: Wiley.

Schank, R.C. (1982) - 'Dynamic Memory'. Cambridge: Cambridge University Press.

Schank, R.C. & Abelson, R. (1977) - 'Scripts, Plans, Goals, and Understanding'. Hillsdale, NJ: Erlbaum.

Schank, R.C., & Colby, K.M. (eds) (1973) - 'Computer Models of Thought and Language'. San Francisco: Freeman.

Schegloff, E. & Sacks, H. (1973) - 'Opening up closings'. Semiotica, 8, 289-327.

Schmandt, C. (1985) - 'Voice Communication with Computers'. In Hartson, H. R. (ed) 'Advances in Human-Computer Interaction I'. New Jersey: Ablex.

Schroeder, M.R. (ed) (1985) - 'Speech and Speaker Recognition, Bibliotheca Phonetica, No. 12'. Basel: Karger.

Schulert, A.J., Rogers, G.T. & Hamilton, J.A. (1985) - 'ADM - A Dialog Manager'. In 'Proceedings of CHI'85 - Conference on Human Factors in Computing Systems'. Association for Computing Machinery, New York. (Published in Europe as L.Borman and B.Curtis (eds) - 'Human Factors in Computing Systems II'. Amsterdam: North-Holland.)

Schwab, E.C., Nusbaum, H.C. & Pisoni, D.B. (1985) - 'Some Effects of Training on the Perception of Synthetic Speech'. Human Factors, 27 (4), 395-408.

Scully, C. (1984) - 'Speaker-Specific Patterns for Articulatory Synthesis'. Proceedings of the Institute of Acoustics, 6, 417-424.

Searle, J.R. (1969) - 'Speech Acts'. Cambridge: Cambridge University Press.

Searle, J.R. (1976) - 'The classification of illocutionary acts'. Language in Society, 5, 1-24.

Shallice, T. (1975) - 'On the contents of primary memory'. In P. M. A. Rabbitt, & S. Dornic (eds), 'Attention and Performance', vol.5. London: Academic Press.

Silverman, K. (1985) - 'What can be done to improve the intonation in synthetic speech ?'. In 'Proceedings of the 11th Symposium on Human Factors in Telecommunications'. Cesson-Sevigne, France: CCETT.

Simon, J.C. (ed) (1980) - 'Spoken Language Generation and Understanding'. Dordrecht: Reidel.

Simpson, C.A. (1982) - 'Evaluation of Synthesised Voice Approach Callouts (SYNCALL)'. In 'Manned System Design', Marael & Kraiss (eds). Plenum Press, New York.

Slowiaczek, L.M. & Nusbaum, H.C. (1985) - 'Effects of Speech Rate and Pitch Contour on the Perception of Synthetic Speech'. Human Factors, 27(6), 701-712.

Sorensen, J.M., & Cooper, W.E. (1980) - 'Syntactic Coding of Fundamental Frequency in Speech Production'. In R.A.Cole (ed), 'Perception and Production of Fluent Speech'. Hillsdale, NJ: Erlbaum.

Stephens, J. & Beattie, G. (1986) - 'Turn-taking on the telephone: textual features which distinguish turn-final and turn-medial utterances'. Journal of Language and Social Psychology, 5, 211-222.

Stewart, T.F.M. (1980) - 'Communicating with Dialogues'. Ergonomics, 23, 909-919.

Taft, M. and Forster, I.I. (1975) - 'Lexical storage and retrieval of prefixed words'. Journal of Verbal Learning and Verbal Behavior, 14, 638-647.

Talbot, M. (1985) - 'Speech Technology: is it Working ?'. In Johnson, P. & Cook, S. (eds) 'People and Computers, Designing the Interface'. Cambridge: Cambridge University Press.

Talbot, M. (1987) - 'What can Human Factors offer the speech-based Human-Computer Interface ?'. In 'Proceedings of International Speech Tech '87'. New York: Media Dimensions Inc.

Tanner, P. & Buxton, W. (1983) - 'Some Issues in Future User Interface Management System (UIMS) Development'. IFIP Working Group 5.2, Workshop on user Interface Management, Seeheim, W Germany, November.

Tate, A. (1976) - 'Project Planning Using a Hierarchic Non-Linear Planner'. Research Report, DAI, University of Edinburgh.

Taylor, R.M. (1986) - 'Integrating Voice, Visual and Manual Transactions: Some Practical Issues from Aircrew Station Design'. Paper presented at the NATO workshop on the structure of multi-modal dialogues including voice. Venaco, France, Sept. 1-5.

Thorndike, E.L. & Lorge, I. (1944) - 'The Teacher's Book of 30,000 Words'. New York: Teachers College Press.

Tyler, L.K., & Marslen-Wilson, W.D. (1977) - 'The on-line effects of semantic context on syntactic processing'. Journal of Verbal Learning and Verbal Behaviour, 16, 683-692.

Underwood, M. J. (1980) - 'What the Engineers would like to know from the Psychologists'. In Simon (1980).

Underwood, K. & Richards, M.A. (1984) - 'How are people naturally inclined to speak to machines ?'. In 'Proceedings of the Ergonomics Society Annual Conference'. London: Taylor and Francis.

van Dijk, T.A. (1977) - 'Text and Context'. London: Longman.

Visick, P. , Johnson, P. and Long, J. (1984) - 'A comparative analysis of keyboards and voice recognition in a parcel sorting task'. In 'Proceedings of the Ergonomics Society Annual Conference'. London: Taylor and Francis.

Voiers, W.D. (1983) - 'Evaluating Processed Speech Using the Diagnostic Rhyme Test'. Speech Technology Magazine, 1, (4), 30-40.

Wasserman, A.I. & Shewmake, D.T. (1983) - 'A RAPID/USE Tutorial'. Laboratory of Medical Information Science, University of California, San Francisco.

Waterworth, J.A. (1982) - 'Man-Machine Speech "Dialogue Acts"'. Applied Ergonomics, 13, 203-207.

Waterworth, J.A. (1983) - 'Effect of intonation form and pause durations of automatic telephone number announcements on subjective preference and memory performance'. Applied Ergonomics, 14, 39-42.

Waterworth, J.A. (1984) - 'Interaction with machines by voice: a telecommunications perspective'. Behaviour and Information Technology, 3, 163-177.

Waterworth, J.A. (1985) - 'The Cognitive Effort of Processing Synthetic Speech'. In 'Proceedings of 11th International Symposium on Human Factors in Telecommunications'. Cesson-Sevigne, France: CCETT.

Waterworth, J.A., & Holmes, W.J. (1986) - 'Understanding Machine Speech'. Current Psychological Research and Reviews, 5, 228-245.

Waterworth, J.A., & Thomas, C.M. (1985) - 'Why is synthetic speech harder to remember than natural speech?'. In 'Proceedings of CHI'85 - Conference on Human Factors in Computing Systems'. Association for Computing Machinery, New York. (Published in Europe as L.Borman and B.Curtis (eds) - 'Human Factors in Computing Systems II'. Amsterdam: North-Holland.)

Watkins, M.J., & Watkins, O.C. (1974) - 'Processing of recency items for free recall'. Journal of Experimental Psychology, 102, 488-493.

Weber, R. P. (1985) - 'Basic Content Analysis'. Beverly Hills, California: Sage.

Whitefield, A.D. (1984) - 'A model of the engineering design process derived from Hearsay-II'. In 'Proceedings of Interact '84: First IFIP Conference on Human- Computer Interaction'. Amsterdam: Elsevier.

Wickelgren, W.A. (1969) - 'Context-sensitive coding, associative memory, and serial order in (speech) behaviour'. Psychological Review, 76, 1-15.

Wickens, C. D. & Vidulich, M. (1982) - 'Stimulus-Central Processing-Response Compatibility and Dual Task Performance in Two Complex Information Processing Tasks: Threat Evaluation and Fault Diagnosis'. Technical Report EPL-82-3-/ONR-82-3, Department of Psychology, University of Illinois.

Winograd, T. (1973) - 'A Procedural Model of language Understanding'. In Schank and Colby (1973).

Winograd, T. (1975) - 'Frame Representations and the Declarative-Procedural Controversy'. In Bobrow and Collins (1975).

Woods, W. A., Kaplan, R., & Nash-Webber, B. (1972) - 'The lunar sciences natural language information system: Final report'. BBN Report No. 2378, Bolt, Beranek and Newman, Inc., Cambridge, Mass.

Wright, R.D. & Crossley, P. (1985) - 'A Synthesis Drafting System on a Micro'. In 'Proceedings of the International Conference on Speech Input/Output: Techniques and Applications'. IEE, London.

Index